CHASING Faith AMONG Yaks AND Nomads

A Memoir

Ann Wyse

CENTRAL
ASIA
PUBLISHING

Chasing Faith Among Yaks and Nomads
Ann Wyse
©2022 Central Asia Publishing

This book is a memoir. It reflects the author's present recollections of
experiences over time. Some names and characteristics have been changed,
some events have been compressed, and some dialogue has been recreated.

Images do not represent the actual people or exact places
discussed in this book in order to maintain privacy.

All scripture quotations are taken from The Holy Bible, English
Standard Version. Copyright © 2001 by Crossway, a publishing
ministry of Good News Publishers. All rights reserved.

ISBN 978-616-7998-32-9 (paperback)
ISBN 978-616-7998-33-6 (e-book)

Printed at Kwik Print, Chiang Mai, Thailand

Published by
Central Asia Publishing
https://www. centralasiapublishing.com
contact@centralasiapublishing.com

To Uncle Jim and Aunt Carol,

You were the first to put this dream in my heart,
and then you gave me the pieces I needed to succeed.

This is for you.

For Mary ~
I hope you enjoy this journey
through Tibet. I AM SO GRATEFUL
for your sweet and wonderful
family. Happy reading!
your Oak Park Heights neighbor,
Deb Wyss
AKA "ann wyse"

CHAPTER 1

$\mathcal{I}$ had been in a seven-passenger van, smashed up against a nomadic man who smelled strongly of sour cheese and something quite earthy for twenty-seven hours straight. I am not complaining about the smell, only documenting, for this was precisely the kind of thing I had been hoping for and dreaming of for quite a good number of years by that point.

The Tibetan man's thick robe of sheepskin and tightly woven wool spilled over onto my own body, and his perfectly straight, perfectly white teeth seemed out of place, situated in the middle of a face that looked like it had been working very hard for a very long time with no great option available for washing.

On the other side of me sat Kel, who was the very reason I had found myself in this particular predicament in the first place. She was my ethnically-Tibetan neighbor in the Chinese city of twelve million people where I held a residency permit. Hidden so deep inside of her that I was still slightly skeptical, she was supposedly a village girl hailing from a tiny farming community in one of the remotest places on earth. She was determined that the two of us would make it to her family's homestead in that isolated and distant location, no matter how much finagling and negotiating and solid discomfort it took.

The girl had come to my rescue more than a few times, and I was apt to trust her by this point. She had been my bridge to this new world I had found myself in when I stepped off that plane six months ago as an American.

When I had felt confident that chopsticks would inevitably equal an undesirable weight loss program for me, she had taught me the word for *spoon* in the local dialect, which any Chinese person would have on hand for the occasion of soup.

When I boarded buses to try and arrive at the countless, unique destinations this exotic country had to offer, I would regularly end up lost. Kel taught me how to make the most of the taxi system when this occurred. Better than that, she would frequently accompany me on explorations around my new neighborhood and to places on the outskirts of the vast city in which we lived. This, of course, allowed me significantly less apprehension and many more opportunities.

She taught me how to bargain for needed items. Maybe more importantly than any of these other things, she sat with me on long evenings that I was convinced would be lonely.

In the earliest days after arriving in Asia, I'd look down from my eleventh-story apartment window at night at the hustle and bustle of it all and feel the tiniest tiny I had ever felt in my entire life. But Kel had accepted me for the misfit I was in that Chinese land, making me feel like being so tiny would somehow be okay.

As my luck would have it, she spoke English, which I would

find out was almost entirely unheard of, even in this massive metropolis. She was the closest thing to me I could find in this place where absolutely everything else felt utterly unfamiliar. She was my first real friend, and when she demanded I accompany her to her village, I was thrilled.

We left in the middle of the night from an eerily-empty street corner, just down the road from the skyscraper building where my apartment door was located across the hall from hers.

I had never seen the city's pavement uncongested, let alone deserted. The daytime hours provided so few empty spaces on these sidewalks that I generally had to keep pace with the moving throng of people just to make my way to my destination.

But tonight, we were alone.

Well, not completely alone because there were more people than could fit in the parked vehicle on the upcoming street corner, crowding around the van's open door. Or so I wrongly thought. You can fit way more than you could ever imagine in a tiny van because after all of our bodies were arranged just so, bags of supplies were then loaded into the cracks of us. We sucked in our tummies, and off we went.

It was the dead of winter, and the run-down van windows remained completely open the entire way. I thought maybe they were broken, as that would have fit the state of the rest of the vehicle, but in the end, I learned that this is the way the nomad travels to and from civilization to buy supplies no matter what the temperature or season.

The trip could have taken as little as twenty-three hours, but the driver, whom I would later find out did NOT have a driver's license, had taken a wrong turn, and two hours later we ended up back where we started. With no one grumbling, no one hardly flinching, we began again.

My young, healthy body ached terribly after tossing and lurching on the partially-completed roads through and around the mountains. The pressure in my head from the steep, high-altitude climb felt like it might lead to the contents of my stomach needing to overflow up and out at any given moment. I was entirely unprepared for that potential problem and was concerned and slightly frantic.

Kel, who had turned into my ridiculously giddy traveling companion, seemed completely unfazed. She kept laughing, joking and slapping me on the back. Giggling seemed like the wrong response to someone in such a situation, no matter how grand the current adventure promised to be. I was hoping she could find me a plastic bag or even a shoe and yell up to the driver to pull over. But of course, she was distracted because she was returning home for the biggest holiday of the year, and it's hard to put a damper on that, no matter how much vomit may be involved.

She was the pride of the village and was returning not only to celebrate the new year but to be celebrated herself. She had made it into the outside world and had gotten a real education. Now, she was a city girl with jeans and a sweater replacing her traditional robes and brightly- colored scarves. Her hair hung loosely down her back in stark contrast to the braids wrapped tightly around the heads of the village girls. A cell phone in hand and makeup permanently tattooed on her face, she was transformed, and she was looking forward to being the envy of all of the girls back home. Her new status meant she carried responsibilities as well, many of them gifts to be given out from her large suitcase that was hopefully still strapped to the top of our moving vehicle.

Little did I know, she had also brought some entertainment. A foreigner with freckles on her face to touch and hair on her arms to explore, and stories from so far away that no one had any idea whether to believe them. A person who sure seemed like a doctor, but who repeatedly said that she was not, while at the same time carrying medicine for pain and sunscreen to protect your skin and chapstick to heal lips. She even had a weird contraption to rub under your armpits to make you smell like wildflowers.

So there we were, twenty-seven hours into our journey, when suddenly, with absolutely no apparent warning, the van jolted to a neck-breaking stop. The endless, happy chatter from my nomad seatmate ceased, and for a moment, it felt like we were suspended in the middle of outer space, in a sea of blackness and total silence. The darkness was so complete that I had no idea if we were in the middle of the road or had fallen off the road, or even if we had somehow hit something.

I held my breath until I noticed a light coming from some-where. A tiny dot slowly got larger and larger until there stood before us a creature unlike anything I had ever seen before. Beautifully wild, with thick, black, shiny hair that extended in and around every direction of her head. Leathery skin, with a still, sculpture-like expression. Huge eyes taking me in. A swollen belly under layers of a robe and an added sheepskin

5

tied around her waist. Soiled face, dirty hands. A flashlight in her hand, which seemed impossible. Surely they must not have things like flashlights in this other world.

Because I had made it, I was here.

I had arrived in the very heart of Tibet.

The white-washed mud house loomed massive behind this exquisite woman, and she beckoned us out of the van and in. I heard soft animal noises through the door but couldn't see well enough to know where the animals were located. I clung to Kel as we climbed strange-feeling stairs, which felt at the same time solid but also with more give than was expected, a very unsettling sensation. The flashlight bounced aside to reveal that the second floor mainly was a gaping hole down to what was below.

I trod carefully.

The silence was also unnerving me. Do these people talk? There had been no hellos, no exchange of sound.

Then again, did it matter? I wouldn't understand them anyway.

We stepped over a threshold, and there we were, inside the central part of the home. A single, exposed lightbulb dangled on a wire, and I felt myself relax, having a bit of control put back into my hands now that I could see.

A man so skinny and so strong looking sat with his legs crossed, smoking a cigarette. His weather-beaten face was welcoming, not shocked by this pale-skinned foreigner who stood before him. He smiled with his whole face and made me feel like a wanted guest.

Someone from behind ushered me in to sit on a twin-sized

bed enveloped on three sides by a highly colorful and ornate headboard. I was careful to sit at the edge not to disturb the sleeping child nestled among the sheepskins behind me. I was also told that this is the polite way to sit, acknowledging that this is not your home and therefore not getting *too* comfortable—an easy way to show respect.

Winter in the mountains of Tibet is frigid, and we warmed ourselves around the blackened and oily-looking wood-burning stove. More accurately, it was dung, not wood—a dung-burning stove.

Salted butter tea was poured from an ancient-looking silver kettle, and even though I was unsure if I could manage to put anything in my still nauseous and roiling belly, I reached for the cup.

Because this was my moment, this was the moment I had been waiting for through what had felt like forever.

In the middle of snow-capped mountains and hills dotted with yaks and tents and fields full of barley, I could finally see that these people I had loved from so far away actually existed.

I smiled with quite possibly the most genuine smile of my life, lifted my cup, and greeted them with the few words I could say in their language, "Happy New Year."

CHAPTER 2

*Y*ou would have thought I had just won an Olympic medal with the burst of applause that followed my first Tibetan words. The cheers, congratulations, and joy that erupted from that room were unmerited.

And, just like that, I had won their hearts, which was wonderful since I had little else to offer. I felt like a newborn, trying to learn how to do everything again. Eating breakfast required skills I had never known. We each received a small ceramic bowl into which I was supposed to concoct a meal by combining my desired ratio of roasted barley flour and butter tea. The mixing process was an art form and involved just one finger and quick scraping motions against the side of the bowl while the other hand twirled the bowl at a rapid, precise, and rhythmic speed. After making a huge mess, I was given additional information on different methods of eating this same breakfast which sounded even more complicated. I guess they had started me out easy.

I even had to be taught how to use the toilet. I'm not joking. At first, I didn't even recognize that the bathroom was a bathroom. There was no door, just three small, hardened-dirt walls that went up to my waist, with a rectangular hole chiseled into the middle of the floor. This was located on the second level of the home, allowing the waste to fall to the home's ground level, next to the animal's quarters. They did not let me enter the bathroom alone, which did feel enormously awkward. Someone was always tasked with the unfortunate job of carrying the flashlight and pointing it directly at me as I used the facilities. I am thankful this prevented me from falling into the hole after dark.

The Tibetan people are the most hospitable people I have ever met. That vibrant and generous village truly embraced me, included me in everything, and gave me so many precious first experiences that I hold so close to my heart, even all of these years later.

I milked a yak for the first time. I carried a basket on my back and collected fresh yak dung to fuel the fires. I learned how to form the dung patties and place them in the sun to dry. I helped carry stones for a village house being constructed and learned how to pound mud for another structure.

I chuckled with delight at translated questions such as "do you use yak dung to make the fires in your village? Is America in India? Are you a nomad? A yak herder? Could you speak English when you were small?" We munched from the snack bowl of fried dough and dried yak meat while Grandma wet-nursed the baby.

The feeling I was experiencing was one of contentment,

satisfaction, and fulfillment. I had lived and breathed and waited and prepared for this moment. To be here, right now, felt worth every single sacrifice I had made along the way. No regrets. No doubts. No hesitation. I was living my dream. I had never felt more sure that this was where I was supposed to be.

That feeling of being in the exact, right place at the exact, right time by God's perfect grace was extremely helpful. Especially when it was announced that it was time for all of us women to head to the hot springs for the once-a-year bath. Getting naked in front of anyone is hugely daunting, but when you are the only white woman anyone has ever seen, there's a bit of extra pressure. The hike to get there was a long and lively procession, and I immensely enjoyed myself as the happiness that spilled out from all of those around me felt contagious.

The cove itself was breathtaking. Towering jagged mountain peaks surrounded us while small waterfalls cascaded down various stacks of rocks around the pool's edges. There was a cave with a large open mouth, providing some shelter from the wind, and the warmth of the water was such a relief from the days of cold.

My fears of being stared at, while warranted, weren't such a big deal. The women were highly discreet in washing, keeping most of their clothes on while giving each other privacy to do what they came to do. Hair washing, however, was a group event, everyone helping everyone to lather on the Tide brand laundry detergent. We were a strong-smelling bunch at the end of that.

In honor of our homecoming, Kel's aging brother-in-law, who I respectfully called Grandfather, dragged in the frozen leg of a yak and hacked off raw pieces for us to enjoy. I didn't pause, as I was such an overly-eager beaver in my newfound surroundings. I popped it into my mouth after covering it with dry spice. After three pieces, I was warned to stop so I didn't get sick. I thought it was probably wise to listen to the locals. But Kel, too excited to be eating her homeland delicacies, carried on for hours.

Suddenly, she grabbed my arm and said she had to go to the bathroom. I held the flashlight while she moaned, grunted, and cried. And that's what we did all night long. In the morning, she was sure she was doomed, and her nephew drove the two of us around on the back of his motorbike, trying to find the village doctor.

When we finally found him, he brought us into the "clinic," which looked like an unused shed, and dug around the cluttered or possibly vandalized shelves to secure a big needle with one hand as he continued smoking with the other. I was alarmed as he filled the syringe and instructed Kel to drop her pants. He swiftly plunged the needle into her tush, and she yelped *very* loudly.

But, then.

It was as if she was instantly healed of any tummy trouble, and we went back home to eat some more raw yak meat.

The following day, it was pitch black as we stumbled into the biting cold at four a.m. This dark thing was just part of life here, I guessed. It would take some time to get used to it. Led only by voices calling to me and a hand I grasped tightly, we made our way to the village monastery.

Culturally, this trip had opened my eyes to so many things, and now I was also getting a dose of Tibetan Buddhism. I was anxious to learn, to see it all firsthand, but I was also scared. Growing up in a pastor's home where the church was all I knew, foreign religions seemed shocking and dangerous.

The altars were particularly eerie in the still night, and the thought of idol worship almost made my blood run cold. The Tibetan gods looked terrifying to me, and the pictures painted on the walls seemed to amplify any unrest in my soul. A mixture between the unknown and the assault I felt they projected on my God made me extraordinarily uneasy and fearful.

I was also unsure where the line should be drawn in my participation in this event. I wanted to be with them during the celebrations that were significant for them. I wanted to show them the respect they deserved as people. But I also had explicitly come to this country and this people and this village to share the hope that I had been given throughout my faith in Jesus.

Jesus and His teachings and this monastery and its gods did not seem to go together.

I had arrived in this country with all of the answers to life's questions tucked securely in my pockets, ready to hand out to anyone and everyone. Still, now that these strangers I had heard about from the other side of the ocean had become real live individuals with personalities and likes and worries and ambitions, I wasn't quite sure exactly how to do that. I was convinced and confident and more than sure that Jesus was worthy of the worship of all people, including those in this gorgeous speck of a place in our great big world. I reveled in the thought of His hope and light and love filling this spot of land, but it all wasn't as simple and straightforward as I had assumed that it would be.

I hung back as they made their offerings with juniper branches and flickering butter lamps, and then I stepped back into the cold night by myself. As the snow formed a thick blanket on my coat, I longed for the animal hides wrapped tightly around me as I slept on the slightly-elevated platform back at Kel's family home. They had cushioned the wooden plank bed with a colorful carpet, then nudged the pallet against the household altar, away from the opening to the outdoors that was only covered with a heavy cloth instead of a solid door.

I tilted my head back to catch a snowflake on my tongue but was stopped short as my breath caught in my throat.

The grandness of the sky enveloped everything.

Stars. Everywhere.

Above, yes, but they also appeared to surround me as I stood with my feet firmly placed on what is generally referred to as the world's rooftop. I stood in that silence alone, in the middle of almost absolutely nowhere, and thought, how did a twenty-six-year-old girl from a suburban town in Minnesota get here?

I felt so insignificant and foolish as I stood there in my long underwear and corduroy pants and borrowed red coat, hoping to make just a little difference for the better somewhere along the way in this lavish, huge, overwhelming world.

What had I been thinking? Why did I think little old me could be up for a task like this? How could I bring Jesus to a people carrying on happily without Him? I wasn't sure where to begin, and I couldn't see how there could ever be an end to that job.

But those thousands of twinkling lights also gently reminded me that God was with me in that exact moment of history. This very story was begun by a God of love and would be finished by a God of love. He had made those stars and decorated that night sky in this particular way and had planted me right here right now. This moment was written in His book. It wasn't by chance that I was here. What role I was to play among these people was uncertain to me, but the fact that I was here now made me part of whatever story He was writing in this sleepy village.

And what *was* certain was that even though I didn't have much, if anything, to offer, God himself had a lot to offer. He could give them anything and everything and do everything and anything. I didn't have anything to worry about because my job was small.

He would be the one doing all of the work.

I just needed to point people in His direction and let them see for themselves.

———

Just after daybreak, we finished circling the monastery, and the job of appeasing the spirits was done for the time being. Just as we were exiting the monastic compound, I felt something hit me in the back. Like a snowball. But not a snowball. It was a fistful of roasted barley flour. And then another. And then fistfuls coming from all directions.

There were hoots and hollers, and men in trees, on mud walls, and hiding behind structures. The barley flour mixed with snow until our hair and coats were a big, slimy mound of dough, and then when we were covered enough, we were required to accompany the growing crowd of barley throwers door to door throughout the village. If the inhabitants didn't open the door to the knocks and yells, they were rewarded by being dragged out of their homes and having their pants stuffed full of the barley. This scene did not grow old, and hours later everyone was still at it.

The Tibetan people's ability to milk joy out of all of the occasions and random minutes of life was astounding. They genuinely seemed carefree and happy. They appeared to have mastered the art of living in the moment and being grateful, which seems to elude the majority of the western world. I wondered if this was an accurate view of these people, but of course, time would be required to observe the cycles of life.

I was prepared to stick it out.

As my time was coming to a close in that place for that time, Grandfather told me that when I returned to my home village in America, he would give me a lamb to take back with me. What a lovely and precious gift from this family who did not have much to offer! When I expressed concern about how I would get it on the plane, he assured me that I could just stick it under my coat for the ride, and no one would notice.

And, I, too, prayed that he would receive the gift of the lamb that I had come to give him. The lamb of God who takes away the sins of the world. Who came and lived amongst man, being full of both grace and truth, and died, in our place, to restore us to the one, authentic, and living God.

I wasn't sure which lamb would end up being harder to receive in the end.

Making their way around the village
monastery during a religious exercise

CHAPTER 3

*D*uring college, I was teased for not being able to hold a conversation after dinnertime due to extreme tiredness. However, out of sheer willpower, I forced myself to sign up for a night class because it was the only time the course "Village Healthcare" was offered. My heart would beat faster with excitement when I thought about what I could learn and how I would use it one day. I felt more than ready to head off into whatever remote location God would place me. I could envision myself out in the mountains or desert or jungle or tundra where I was needed most, where physical and spiritual lives hung in the balance.

The class was three hours long for every session. And, like I'm pretty sure I mentioned, at night. The teacher was a little old woman who still spent half the year in African villages, bringing medical care to the least of these, and boy was she a tough one. The day we learned how to give shots, we were all nervous. She nonchalantly asked us to try it out on each other, making sure to flick the needle so that there was no bubble in the syringe because that could be fatal.

Did she remember she was dealing with amateurs here? And by amateurs, I mean squirrelly, 19-year-old college students. So, she audibly sighed at our resistance, rolled up both sleeves, and had us form two lines. Then we poked her from both sides, one after the other. She was either ready to die or had already been through too much in her life to think she could die from needle pricks in a sanitary US classroom.

We didn't have assigned seating, but as so many of us are creatures of habit, we routinely found our spots the same way each week. I happened to sit next to a very distinct-looking man. He towered over the rest of us, both in stature and life. He was older, with skin that looked worn out and eyes that communicated in one glance that he had seen more of what life could throw at you than all of the rest of us put together. His stance exuded confidence in a way I had not seen before, even though he looked like he was not in the right place.

I found out pretty quickly that his English was not so great. He always leaned over, looking at me to explain what the teacher said in simpler words. It wasn't for lack of desire. The guy had dictionaries sprawled all across his desk. And the script those books contained also looked unlike anything I had ever seen before. What language *was* that?

It turns out; I'd find out soon enough. A few weeks later, he was the guest speaker in a different class of mine. He passionately told us about his homeland, Tibet, in his broken, heavily accented English. He explained how an American woman had moved in among them, learned their language, taught their children, and had shown Him Jesus. He was here to ask us: Will you go to my people and tell them about Jesus?

Before that day, I knew nothing about Tibet. I didn't even know where Tibet was in the world. But as he spoke, my heart felt like it was being squeezed continuously in a distinct and uncomfortable, yet telling, way. From that moment on, I could think of nothing else. At night, when I closed my eyes, I dreamed of that land I had never seen before in such vivid detail that when I awoke, it felt as if I had legitimately lived those images that played out behind my closed eyelids. During the day, I wept for those people and was filled with compassion and love more immense than my own.

Furthermore, I determined that by God's grace, I would go. I would say yes to this man's plea and say yes to God's call to these people.

Four years later, I sobbed my whole way there. Literally. Did you even know it was possible to cry for twenty-eight hours straight? I didn't, and I'm sure the lady sitting next to me on the airplane didn't either.

I had grown up with Jesus feeling like just another family member. Our little house was tucked next to the church building, where we spent hours and days of our lives each week while my daddy preached the Bible and my mom played the piano. Before I said my first word, I had probably heard about my sin and my need for a savior just as much as I had heard about anything else.

Missionaries visited our church not frequently but regularly.

I remember slide shows with pictures from foreign lands and snippets of stories from far away places over pot roast and potatoes cooked up by my mom for Sunday lunch as she served those laborers for the kingdom.

Almost by accident, I found out that teenagers could go on short trips to other countries to tell people about Jesus, too. I launched myself into the middle of those plans just as fast as possible. I couldn't exactly explain it, but I had never wanted anything more.

As much as the idea of foreign lands and ways and places and people were beautifully exotic in an entirely enticing and alluring way, I also felt confident in the role that Jesus should play in the life of everyone, not just me. I believed that God had intricately formed every person on the planet in their mother's womb and desired a real relationship with each one. I thought Jesus was the only way to accomplish that. I had no qualms about speaking that truth to others, and more than that, I felt compelled to share the gospel, this good news, with others.

After my first cross-cultural experience in Mexico, I was hooked. By the following year, after a second experience, I was pretty confident that this was what I wanted to do with my life and what God wanted me to do with my life.

A few things were probably at work in this decision. I think my natural interests provided more than a nudge to get me into cross-cultural and intercultural ministry. My favorite subjects in school were foreign languages. I loved to travel. New situations thrilled me rather than intimidated me. I think God made me that way on purpose. I also believe His additional prodding made me take the big and final plunge.

Also, my faith was growing - slowly and clumsily - but steadily. I cared more about God's fame than the promise of adventure that foreign work seemed to carry. I also loved God enough and knew Him enough that I desired worship of Him to spring up among all of the nations. I was ready to give my life for that cause.

My parents probably had more to do with me going into a ministry life than they realized. They had given their lives for the gospel, serving and starting churches to reach those who didn't have the living hope of peace that came through Jesus. They had been an example to me of loving any and all kinds of people. They emphasized meeting both physical and spiritual needs, which often looked like sharing meals and time and money with others. They visited prisons and nursing homes, and hospitals. They opened up our home on holidays for those who didn't have a place to go. They picked up hitchhikers along the road and shared sidewalks and conversations with drug addicts. They accidentally or purposefully taught me and showed me that all people have value and are worthy of respect and love, and what better way to help them than to give them Jesus.

So, when my mom practically begged and pleaded with me not to become a global worker sent out by the church because it meant I would move so very far away, I found it ironic because I think my parents' way of life had almost as much to do with my final decision as either God or I did.

The decision was easy. More accurately, it did not feel like a decision at all but rather a knowing. Like it had been lying underneath the surface of me for my whole existence, just waiting to emerge. Then, after what I like to call my lightning bolt experience when I heard about Tibet, I was all in.

I was young. I was inexperienced. I was impulsive. Not exactly the best combination. But I was also passionate and teachable. I also had God on my side, even if ignorance was trailing not far behind.

And so I disembarked from the plane on the other side, face swollen, eyes stained red, my few worldly possessions I had chosen to keep squeezed into my suitcase, into a whole new ballgame called China.

CHAPTER 4

I attended school each day to learn Chinese. I went to a university expressly set up for the minority peoples within China that also included programs inserted haphazardly for foreigners such as myself. My classmates hailed from numerous countries around the world.

While showing up at university was a prerequisite by the government for me to keep my residency permit, it was also the best place for me. In a country with over 1 billion Chinese speakers, I would need to speak Chinese, even though the Tibetans I came to reach spoke a completely unrelated language. Being derived from different origins and placed into separate language families, Mandarin Chinese and the Tibetan language were about as different as different could be.

I learned my numbers in Chinese and practiced saying "how much?" over and over. I realized that I wasn't very self-conscious about making language mistakes, which was a gift in my current environment, which required me to constantly use what I was learning to get to the end of each day. It also gave me the freedom to talk to anyone and everyone, which was great practice for beginners. I was not afraid to look silly or stupid, which was good news because I think I looked both of those things on the regular.

I loved the local cuisine and was delighted to find out that there were small restaurants lining every street, and it was also what I considered crazy cheap. I could easily eat lunch out for one USD. I carried around a phrase sheet to help me order, but it often wasn't as easy as I assumed.

One day, I pointed to a phrase that loosely translated as "pork with bean sauce." I tried to say the words aloud while indicating the beautiful characters on the paper.

When the server responded to my request, her words rushed at me, and I didn't understand a single one.

I replied slowly in Chinese, "I'm sorry, I don't understand."

She rolled her eyes and shouted at me, and walked away. I was not sure what we had or had not communicated, but I received a very delicious meal shortly after that exchange. Emboldened by my success, I tried to ask for hot sauce, but instead, I got a bowl of boiling water. Bravely, I tried again and got an extra set of chopsticks. I decided I'd just call that experience a mini-victory and let my failures just be background noise to procuring a meal all on my own.

My apartment was becoming more and more like a home I could enjoy. It was a small one-bedroom that had been very run-down and filthy from lack of use. All of the teal and glitter kitchen cabinets were broken, and there was a huge wet spot covered in mold that took up a large part of one of the walls, while gaping holes littered the other walls. The toilet was not only broken but rotting, and there was not a single closet in the entire home. The home was furnished, but as the space had been initially used as an office, that exclusively meant a thinly padded, stiff couch and matching chairs with multiple rips in the vinyl placed around a solitary, plastic coffee table.

While unsure if this living situation would be worth the effort when I was first shown it by the real estate agent, the enormous, south-facing, almost floor-to-ceiling window in the living room sold me with its promise of any sun and warmth that could get me through the cold winters with no central heat available. Any people living in the country of China below the Yellow River had no options for central heat, even though the winters could be quite brutal.

I had significant help in fixing the place up from other ex-pats and construction workers, who replastered and painted the walls and even built me a closet and shelves. I tried to make it my own by covering up the giant mural painted into the tile in the kitchen—an oversized hamburger and saxophone decorated half of the wall. I taped pictures from home in its place and bought throw blankets and pillows to soften the only seats in the living room.

When it was all said and done, it was very simple and still on the very rough side compared to American living, but I was content. It even had a washing machine, although I took a major gamble with my clothes on the first attempt at using it. I had no idea what any of the buttons labeled in Chinese meant. My clothes did come out unshrunk and smelling clean, so I considered that one more of a significant victory, and I reminded myself never to bump any of the buttons to risk a change in settings.

I decided there was just one thing missing.

My bright idea was to track down a Tibetan roommate to help me acculturate and learn the Tibetan language more quickly, even though my focus was studying the Chinese language. A completely unrelated language, remember. I had high hopes that studying two foreign languages simultaneously would work out okay.

I found my roommate by prayer and impulsivity. I climbed apartment stairs and wandered through hallways looking for open doors. I'm not talking about spiritual open doors. I mean literal, open doors. Tibetans seem to have much more community spirit than us westerners, and some apartment doors would remain open during the day. Peeking my head in and saying hello generally brought an invitation to tea and an interesting learning experience for me.

So, one day, I prayed for a roommate, and I stuck my head in an open door. Many people were congregated in this makeshift hotel - an apartment full of beds that you could rent individually for a couple of dollars a day.

On this day, I met Jun, and I invited her to live with me free of charge if she taught me the Tibetan language. It was a done deal on the spot. It was as easy as that.

I found a second bed to squeeze into my apartment, and that first night I was shocked to hear the mammoth sound that could be produced from this small Tibetan woman's mouth and nose while she slept. I also quickly learned that the floor was considered a dirty spot in Jun's way of life, and disposing of anything there was fair game….sunflower seed shells spit out of the mouth, snot shot from the nose while closing one nostril, watermelon juice and rinds. There seemed always to be something questionable littering the floor.

I had said the point of this was to learn the customs of my present society, right? Had I bitten off more than I could chew?

Apparently not, because soon after we had somewhat gotten used to each other, one of my new roommate's friends showed up on our doorstep. A real, live, nomad woman.

And one with a heartbreaking story. Her husband had shockingly taken on her own mother as a second wife. While having two wives was not unheard of in Tibet, and having two husbands was even more common, a mother and daughter sharing the same husband was quite unorthodox. And, it was too much. She left her two daughters with her mother and husband and fled to the city, to my doorstep. She needed space to breathe and space to think, and freedom to be.

You don't turn someone away like that who has lost everything. So, we made room for one more, and over time, she also found space for smiles. We laughed so hard in between ducking when I tried to teach them how to use forks and knives, and they laughed at my attempts to speak Chinese and Tibetan. I had never seen silverware fly so far across a room, and they had never heard such ridiculous sounds come out of someone's lips. They also got me to make sheep brains a regular part of my diet.

During this season, I marveled at how small my place was in God's plans but how ordained God's great story was. One night, before bed, Jun said, "I started studying the Bible." My language skills were pretty basic then, and I was sure I had misheard her.

I hadn't misheard her.

A Korean woman was teaching her the Bible. To this day, I don't know how it happened or who the Korean woman was, but God was at work.

Another day, Jun's family was visiting from the mountains, and we were all having a meal together in our shared home. Jun's twelve-year-old niece was shyly trying a bite of homemade pizza for the first time when Jun motioned toward her and said, "She believes like you."

And she did. She was a Christian. A Tibetan Christian. In my living room. There were maybe a handful of these people in existence, and here was one randomly in my living room, visiting from her home in the distant mountains.

Or maybe it wasn't so random.

But how? She had been given the opportunity to attend a boarding school run by foreigners, heard about Jesus' power over sin, evil, and death, and surrendered her life to him.

Her faith was new, but she had taken a stand amongst her family, and they had allowed it. She was not permitted to tell other people that she had a different faith, but they allowed her to practice her new religion in their home.

This fact was made even more remarkable because her slightly younger brother was one of very few believed to be a reincarnate Buddhist god. He had grown up in the monastery, being whisked away from his family at a young age when it was revealed that he was a living god to be taught the ways of the

Tibetan high monks. His authority was unquestioned, and he even had a grown man as a servant who slept at the foot of his bed and attended to his every need and want. He was revered for hundreds of miles around and would have visitors arriving on horseback at all hours of the day and night to pay their respects and worship him, bringing him gifts in exchange for a blessing and advice for their future steps.

Now, all of us were crowded around a single card table. A Tibetan boy dressed in priestly robes, worshipped by the masses. An American young woman, fresh out of college and trying to love and honor Jesus in a foreign land. A Tibetan village mama tending to her fields, livestock, and children day after day. A young woman trying her luck at city life and living with an American. And a twelve-year-old girl attending boarding school who was learning about Jesus.

Here we were, together.

An odd crew. But a perfectly crafted crew. They belonged to me, and I belonged to them. I wasn't willing to say this was a co-incidence. We had been brought together to live, learn, grow, and love. And that's precisely what we did over the following years.

And so it was that the Tibetan world became more and more my world amid that big Chinese city. Soon all of my friends were Tibetans, and Chinese life mainly was something I was forced to navigate when I needed groceries or needed to mail a letter.

My co-workers existed alongside me as well, but my inter-actions with them seemed few and far between in comparison with the Tibetan world, which at first was a pill I found hard to swallow. As a single, I had hoped and believed I would be working daily beside my teammates, but that was not exactly practical or realistic or even the best in this life. I came to understand the enormous blessing it was to be forced early on to be so interconnected with those I had come to reach, and, in time, I came to understand that those teammates would always have my back, which would be needed. They were just busy plowing ahead with all that their own full and meaningful lives entailed, and that didn't always include the new girl tagging along. The rhythms of my relationships with other workers in the field got easier to navigate the further down the path we walked, and we were forged together with fire more than a time or two.

There is one co-worker of note I would like to mention. He was the only other lone single under the age of sixty in our group, and so someone I tended to gravitate towards, never mind that he also happened to be on the handsome side. At twenty-five, he had already been in China for two-and-a-half years before I arrived.

On paper, we should have hit it off easily, but my first interaction with him left me baffled. When I asked him what his plans were for the upcoming week, he replied, and I quote:

"Probably turn off my lights, lock my door, eat pizza, and watch movies."

Honestly, that was not the correct answer if he was trying to impress me, which, to be fair, I'm quite certain he had no desire to do. He was a tired, introverted guy who had just spent two months traveling through Tibet's roughest and toughest parts, speaking only strange and foreign languages, eating nothing but strange and foreign foods, and living out of a backpack in the homes of country villagers and nomads. To be even more clear:

He hadn't had one single moment to himself in two months. It might be about time that he had a bit of a break before starting all over again.

But I just couldn't understand. Not that early on in my story. I was there to pour myself out for the lost, and pizza was not part of the program. But it would be. Because there comes the point when you realize that to make it for the long haul, something has to give.

In a couple of years, I would know the feeling that provoked this startling response from that young man. I would understand that sometimes you needed to rest in a way that felt like real rest.

This was no 9-5 job, that was for sure.

Many other foreign workers became nothing short of family. Still, their stories are their own to tell, and I have purposefully left their words and actions behind while intentionally carrying their echoes in my heart through these pages. They are the heroes of those years, and I learned so much from them. They have and will always have my sincerest affections.

It was a wild life. The days rolled out fresh with surprise, never being able to guess what might wait just around the corner. In the beginning, I think I can say I almost enjoyed that aspect of this new way of life.

CHAPTER 5

*L*ike that time, late one night, I heard a pounding at my door so fast and furious and noisy that I dumped hot chocolate on my computer keyboard. With a racing heart, I opened the door to a group of men in army fatigues yelling loudly as they pushed past me into my living room. Not understanding a word they said, I watched as they opened my living room window, tied ropes to the railings, and began to rappel down the side of the building. Just as soon as they arrived, they were gone.

I still don't have any idea what that was about.

Another night, I awoke to a massive cockroach stuck in my hair. As I screamed and pulled and got it out, I threw back my covers to find another one in my sheets. And then I resigned myself to the fact that I was not in Kansas anymore.

One unexpected experience that I could never have bargained for was when I accidentally met a very famous Tibetan pop star by force. It had been a long week, and I put on some cozy PJs and settled in for the night. I was ready to crash.

But I was starting to learn that even bedtime was not something that could be counted on.

There was yet again a loud pounding on the door. Why was it always so urgent-sounding? I opened the door to find a woman named Loma decked out in an outrageous get-up, talking a million miles a second. As I wasn't getting what she was saying fast enough for her liking, she started pulling my arm and dragging me behind her out into the hallway.

"Slow down," I said.

"I need your help," she said. "With my boss."

"Now?" I said.

"Right now!" she said.

I actually said no. One of my first times saying no since moving to China. I was depleted. This girl was a total wild card. I never knew what she was up to, and most of the time, it wasn't anything good as I had been slow to learn through past encounters. It seemed she was not afraid to do whatever might prove to work out to her benefit in some way down the road. I just didn't have the energy to keep up with her that night.

But I lost the battle.

She wore me down, and I found myself getting dressed at ten p.m. and waiting on the side of the road for a taxi with her.

The taxi ride was long, and I felt angry. She had promised me this favor would be quick. And, of course, it wasn't.

As we got out of the taxi in the middle of downtown nightlife, she said, "Pretend I speak English." A plot twist. Naturally.

We were greeted at the studio by the big man himself. One of the most famous singers in Tibet and well known all over China.

He towered over us in both height and belly, and his cowboy hat and long hair made him even bigger. Truly a larger-than-life character.

Loma introduced us, then looked at me and said, "Abaka la OObb baBuba lo fa." Ah, so this was how she planned to impress her boss with her excellent English skills. My annoyance was turning to incredibility. And, so, what was there to say in response?

I said, "Ba na wet pa pa tooey."

Everyone smiled and nodded in agreement.

I was whisked onto an ornate set, handed headphones, and placed in front of a studio microphone with an English script. I was to read this poetic verse over the music for the singer's newest CD, set to hit the shelves in the US and England. But lo and behold, the script was anything but poetic. It had been translated into English by someone who did not speak English. An hour later, I had whipped it up into something understandable, and then I began to read.

In the wee small hours of the morning, I finally crawled into my bed and slept for a couple of hours.

In the morning, I succumbed to my American upbringing, and I started the coffee pot as soon as I got out of bed, just before seven. With a full traveler's mug in hand, I headed down to the bike shed to pick up my trusty but rusty, bright-blue bike and proceeded to ride the less than ten minutes to my Chinese language class at the university, which began promptly at 8 a.m.

As I zipped down the road among the thousands of other bicyclists, the sound of countless men and women clearing their throats filled my ears.

On-campus, students made a mad dash for class with meat dumplings in their hands, trying to finish breakfast on the go. I entered my classroom and squeezed my small body into the almost-too-small desk, and felt compassion for the 6-foot 4-inch classmate to my left, who was sitting crookedly with his legs sprawled across the aisle, as there was nowhere else for them to go.

The teacher began giving a grammar lesson in Chinese to the ten of us who were enrolled to learn Mandarin at the beginning level. If I didn't know any better, I would have thought the teacher was yelling at us, but Chinese tends to sound a bit abrasive as it incorporates high pitches and harsh tones, especially if your teacher is as passionate as mine was.

At break, my classmate and I walked to the foreign affairs office to check the big stack of mail delivered a few times a week. As we dug through the bin of letters, we searched for our names to jump out at us amidst the thick, scattered pile. We hoped for any tidbit of happiness that may reach us from home. I never knew I would so look forward to all of the small things: hearing about who got a haircut, what garage sale find my mom had scored, or how well a new recipe turned out in the end. It made the 7,000 miles between us feel minuscule for those moments I sat curled up in the hallways with the paper between my fingers.

We also used the trough toilet at the break, a long rectangle that we all squatted over. There was never any toilet paper or soap for public use, and I quickly got used to remembering to carry my own wherever I went.

After school, I returned my bike to the shed, paying the required fee to the woman who sat there all day long, keeping watch and making sure no one stole my bike or the hundreds of others she was responsible for. She even had a little room right there, with a bed for sleeping and a hot plate for cooking meals and making tea.

While I'm thinking of it, a fascinating cultural tidbit is that you also need to pay for using public bathrooms in China.

I then climbed aboard a bus to hit up a bigger grocery store for a stock up, rather than the markets and smaller stores near my home where I more often shopped. I tried to reach for a pole overhead quickly before the bus lurched back onto the road, although I was so sandwiched between two people that I don't think it mattered much.

A trip to the store probably seems mundane, but for me, it never was. I always seemed to break some rules that I was not aware of. Once, I took a picture to send home to my mom so she could see how different Chinese grocery stores were compared to what we had in my hometown. Before my elbows were even lowered, multiple men surrounded me, asking me to hand over my camera.

Sometimes I would have so many people trying to help me that I could not even *see* the item I was trying to purchase on the shelf. Other times, when I would walk toward a sales clerk, they bolted the other way. Maybe they were afraid I was going to speak English to them.

Trying to get my produce or meat weighed by the attendant made my heart pound wildly, as there was no system for lining up that I could figure out in my American lens of viewing the world. The customers instead jockeyed and elbowed their way closer to the scale, and this competition was one I was very uncomfortable joining. We would then need to thrust our products of choice onto the metal platform quicker than the other hands trying to do the same thing.

The meat itself was splayed out in piles, no wrapping or packaging, but just big metal spoons and tongs we all took turns sharing as we filled up plastic bags with whatever we planned to make for dinner later that night.

I often tried to buy an item that I didn't know what it was to try out new things. That was never hard to accomplish, as my illiteracy made it impossible to decipher many items such as bottles of sauces, cleaning supplies, or snacks.

I had quite a bit of stuff on the way home, so I decided to take a cab rather than the bus. My driver was relentlessly puffing on a cigarette that was coming to an end, but there was another one to follow immediately. Now that the city had officially passed a law that all people in the front row must wear a seat belt, the taxi drivers willingly placed the belt on their stomachs but never moved on to fasten them.

At home again, it was time to study. My tutor arrived, and we worked our way through the day's lesson, but only after she searched through all of my groceries and demanded the price of each one. She then railed against me at how I had paid too much again. Would I ever learn?

Before supper, I went for a run. I'd go for a run several times a week. Or maybe more accurately, a jog. A slow jog. I have never been athletic. What I really mean is that I was a resident bench warmer on the B squad for any sport I decided to try and play. However, I felt an obligation to do something to keep myself alive, and running was the easiest and fastest thing that seemed to accomplish that goal. So, although I dreaded getting myself out the door for this unpleasant activity, I did it a lot.

I had started by jogging at the dirt track at my host school. It always amused me as I ran past men in their business suits and women in dresses and heels RUNNING around the track. Who would have ever thought I'd be out of place in sweats on a track? Even as I dodged soccer games, college students making out, older men doing moves reminiscent of The Karate Kid, and students in military fatigues shouting out communist party slogans, I found the track one of the more peaceful places I encountered on an average day.

But like most places in China, the track had been placed under construction, so I was forced to run the streets of China instead if I was going to get a run in. It meant that the things I needed to dodge were of a different variety. Double-decker busses, bicycle rickshaws, vendors, dogs, more dogs, dogs, and about four million people.

Interestingly enough, I never had to dodge another runner. They seemed not to exist, and I was probably right in that assumption by the stares I got. But answer me this: how can twenty older women, wearing flashy, matching outfits and dancing around with swords in their hands, not turn ONE HEAD,

but a single runner was out of place enough that people stopped what they were doing to watch?

With the arrival of the evening, I went back to school again, but this time in the role of teacher. I enjoyed teaching English so much that I carried on with it in some form or another for my entire time in China. The students were so eager to improve their English that you couldn't help but want to help them reach their dreams. They were very expressive when they spoke English, with exaggerated syllables and facial expressions. They talked much louder in English than when they spoke in Tibetan, and they loved to try and use slang to prove their competence.

I would often wonder how they picked their English names! Some of my favorite names used by people along the way: Piglet, Blue Shoes, Tornado, and Bunny. I sometimes decided to have some fun and follow in their footsteps. I would introduce myself in low-key and appropriate situations with various interesting Chinese names such as Coca-Cola and Snow White.

On the walk home from teaching, I passed Tibetans everywhere in this pocket of the city. It was known as the Tibetan quarters, and the street corners were filled with tough guys, declaring their strength and power with short swords strapped to their belts and big jewelry adorning their chests. There were also gentle mothers with bright scarves used as belts or hairpieces and colorful patterns sewn onto the edges of their robes. Children were toddling along in puffy pants with a large opening between their legs, technically called split pants, which assisted in efficiently managing their bathroom needs without diapers. By the way, it totally works! Older women were thumbing prayer beads and chanting quietly to themselves and their hopeful saviors, while smiling monks strolled by with robes swirling around their trendy sneakers.

Tibetan restaurants lined the streets, boasting meat pies and homemade yogurt. Brothels flashed their lights. Gold-plated idols could be bought for a price. Children and adults who looked the part begged for money. Countless open-air Chinese restaurants were sandwiched between the Tibetan stores, displaying trays of pig ears, snouts, and tails among boiled peanuts and cold vegetable dishes on trays along the sidewalk.

Street food was widely available from vendors and their carts and lived up to its reputation. Sweet potatoes, popcorn, and chestnuts in fall. Fresh flatbread and lamb kabobs year-round. Soy milk, sweet buns, and steamed dumplings filled with pork in the morning. And, of course, there is stinky tofu whenever you happen to be unlucky. That's the real, official name. And that's the real, official smell.

I stopped at the little shop next to my house to buy an ice cream on a stick. The shopkeeper knew my favorite kind was vanilla with chocolate coating, and he told me before I even opened the freezer that he was all out. He tried to sell me a green pea ice cream instead, but I settled for a yogurt popsicle, which he put on my tab. I told him that one day I was going to run the shop to give him a day off, and he looked amused but also like he probably wouldn't trust me. Fair enough.

I went back to my apartment for the night, but Chinese study was not yet done, as my roommate was in the mood for some chit-chat.

When it was finally time to hit the sack, the noises of the city filled my small room. Horns honking, TVs blaring, a domestic fight, rock music pumping through the speakers from a store down the road, and security guards shouting.

It was a loud place, but the sounds were becoming familiar, a feeling I was okay with getting used to.

This was my home.

CHAPTER 6

*C*ity life was only part of the equation in my life overseas. Trips to Tibetan mountainous regions were constants, and I never spent too long in the city before venturing out over any breaks from school.

Returning to Kel's village became almost a habit, and as I weaved my way through Nangla, I heard shouts of greeting from those out tending to their work and their children. As I reached Kel's family home, Grandfather told me that another grandchild had been born just a few days earlier. I found this incredibly interesting, as when I had asked Kel about when her sister-in-law's baby was due the last time we had visited, Kel looked at me strangely and said, she's not pregnant. Well, amongst a million other things, I would come to learn that talking about pregnancy is entirely and utterly taboo in this fascinating culture.

So, here we were with a brand-new baby boy. Both mother and baby were fine - delivered in the barn with the help of Grandmother to keep the mess out of the central part of the house.

The highest religious leaders in Buddhism, called lamas, had come to perform a cleansing ceremony for the new baby after the difficult journey of being reborn into the world. The ceremony was complete with loud, monotonous-sounding chanting and the beating of drums in the sacred prayer room of the house, a space I had never been allowed to enter. They prayed for wisdom to be imparted to the child, for evil to be warded off, and for health. They asked me to hold and keep watch over the baby for the duration of this ceremony.

These bizarre occurrences of being present for intimate and important rituals that clashed with my religious beliefs kept happening. They were way more commonplace than I expected, liked, or hoped for. It made for much awkwardness in my soul and in the actual physical room or wherever I happened to be. It called for quick thinking, decision-making, and follow-through that often felt too tricky to navigate with my limited knowledge and experience, and I found myself floundering.

The sounds coming from the other room sounded ominous and dark, but the sunlight filtered warmly and brightly in through the window, and the baby gurgled and nestled and was content in my arms, which made the random combination of light and darkness and peace and fear mix me all up emotionally inside.

I wasn't sure what to do, so I prayed. I talked to God about what I was thinking and feeling. I prayed about this new life that I was holding that I believed He had formed and fashioned in his mother's womb and had a specific purpose for walking these dusty village paths and narrow mountain trails. And I sat with that boy at that moment as we all thought about his future, where it would lead, and who he would be.

The breathtaking beauty of the mountains just outside of the window made me marvel at what God had made, and then I marveled more that the same God who had made those mountains had also made this little one in my arms.

The Lord would fulfill His purpose for this baby boy. He had promised in His word. The Lord would also meet His purpose for me. He had promised in His word. It felt odd to have these scriptures feel so real and close and strong in the middle of my uncertainty about what was going down in the room next to me and about my place in this situation.

I felt a flicker of His light in my heart, and then His truth overwhelmed me. "The light shines in the darkness, and the darkness shall not overcome it."

He is the light, and He was in me. No matter if I was the only one who carried His light in this place - no matter how small, the darkness - no matter how great, could not overcome it. He was stronger yet.

Why did His presence always feel so strong in these hard places? Was it because I was so desperately aware of my need for Him that His grace covered me with a blanket of His dear nearness?

I didn't know what awaited me or what awaited this little boy, but I knew that God was preparing the way, and that was all that I needed to know to keep moving.

Grandfather quietly told me that he had signed me up for yak herding duty the following morning with a telling smile. The farmers were on a rotation schedule, alternating turns to take all of the villagers' yaks up into the hills to graze.

I stuck close by the side of the one other woman in our group - a nun. The three others - burly, long-haired men - joked and laughed as we climbed higher and higher. The younger of the two proposed marriage to me, and the hoots reached a higher level, and I felt uncomfortable. The nun seemed to have little experience dealing with this, so I was on my own.

The yaks began to spread out and eat, and we plopped ourselves down on a grassy slope that looked out over the tiny dots of homes far off. And then it began to rain. No one mentioned it, but umbrellas were opened. The weather here seemed nothing more than a footnote, and life went on as if nothing had changed.

After a while, the older man, bundled in a wool sweater, found shelter in a cave to make a fire. When it was up and blazing, we joined him, and well-worn leather sacks were opened so we could scoop handfuls of roasted barley flour into our salted butter tea, made with the help of the fire. In the beginning, one bite of "tsampa," which I feel is best described as a healthy breakfast- cereal-tasting ball of playdough, felt like a brick in my stomach. Although still not a welcome sight, I did adapt and learned to eat enough of the dough to feel satisfied and not too queasy.

After lunch, I learned how to yelp a specific high-pitched syllable and twirl a woven, knotted rope to encourage the yaks to move in the direction I desired. I felt pretty confident in my abilities until they sent me down the hillside alone to gather any stragglers. The responsibility of leaving no yak behind made me question the competence I was so proud to possess just moments before. I was concerned even further when the group members pulled their hats over their eyes and laid down for a snooze, leaving me in charge.

Thinking about Jesus as the Good Shepherd while I rubbed shoulders with shepherds and herded yaks and watched them being cared for gave me a new appreciation for the care that God promised and delivered time and time again, even as I wandered away or needed something specific to sustain my very life or just got a bit distracted.

As much as I was thinking about not losing a single yak, someone was thinking of me, too.

The descent back to the village was surprisingly more challenging than going up. The paths felt too small and too steep, and a misstep felt like it could end with me flipping and flopping and flying through too much air before landing at the bottom of the precipice. But when we arrived back, and the farmers met us to collect their hairy livelihoods, I was proud to have taken part in such an integral part of daily life here.

If herding is the epitome of daily life for many Tibetans, tent festivals are the highlight. Everyone sets up a family tent. Or two. You're probably picturing a simple camping tent, but you would be wrong. They are huge. Enormous enough that they *also* move out their actual wooden beds, maybe a few nightstands, definitely their coffee table, and all of the other necessities into these elaborately decorated tents for seven days. Oh. And usually a full-on kitchen. Wood burning stove, you know. Definitely enough space for entertaining lots and lots of guests. Because lots and lots of guests are definitely coming, and the cooking and piling of food begins. The table is stacked. Like maybe two feet high. There are lots of goodies and sweets, dried meat and nuts, beer, and good old-fashioned soda. And then there is mealtime. Steaming stacks of "momos," which are yak meat dumplings dripping with grease, are then dipped into eye-watering spicy deliciousness.

The entertainment is second to none, and the personal space is non-existent. People are smashed together like sardines, and others are crawling as high as they can on top of lumber piles, up trees, and hanging out of the windows and from the rooftop to get a better look at the activities. I have to admit the strong man competition was completely enthralling. Two hundred and fifty pounds of sand were packed into a yak hide bag, and the contestants competed to see who could carry it the furthest. It's always those scrawny guys that win. You know, like those hotdog-eating contests? How it's always the tiny guy that can down the most?

My personal favorite was the tsampa-making contest. Contestants must race to find wood, start a fire, boil water, and make tsampa, their staple food. What adds to the fun is that contestants are allowed to steal, cheat, put out other contestants' fire, and do whatever they want to get the crowd roaring with laughter.

The clothes are flashy, and the talent is on display. Beautiful, intricate, complex, perfectly-synchronized dancing in elaborate and gorgeous costumes. Singing that moves you even if you don't understand a word they say.

The biggest event has got to be the horse races. They have foot races as well, many people barefoot, clamoring their way to the tops of mountains. But the horse races were unlike anything I had ever seen before, decked-out horses with decked-out riders, bending backward to pick up scarves laid out on the ground as the horses galloped at breakneck speeds right next to each other. Every activity is accompanied by eating sunflower seeds. Cracking the shells between the teeth and spitting them out while swallowing the seed. You will not leave a Tibetan horse festival without sunflower seed shells in your hair.

And you won't care. It's that much fun.

My birthday happened to take place during festival week. In a place where no one could tell you what day of the week it was, Kel managed to procure a western-style looking (but not tasting!) cake and taught her family how to celebrate a birthday, which is not something they have ever done before. Look inside a Tibetan's passport here in the US, and I would venture a guess that their birthday is January 1st, and the year is probably just a guess. They don't keep track of things like that.

Watching Tibetans of all ages singing a mumble-jumble version of "Happy Birthday" in literally no language while clapping their hands and laughing hysterically is probably my all-time favorite memory of those years. It was a stepping stone in my journey of learning that it doesn't take much to love another human being, you don't always need language to communicate, and that friendship can most definitely transcend age.

Festival tents

CHAPTER 7

Something I was having a more challenging time genu-inely grasping was Buddhism. This was confounding to me since I was such an intense student when I pored over my world religions courses and eventually studied this particular branch of Buddhism specifically.

Before I arrived, I read about Buddhism and all of its forms. I certainly knew a lot about Buddhism, and I was sure I under-stood Buddhism. But reading about Buddhism and watching it practiced and played out in the actions and rituals and dear-ly-held beliefs in people's real lives felt very different. Completely different.

Viewing Buddhism only through the lens of the Christian faith and the American church made things, dare I say, ridicu-lously oversimplified.

For example, when I was sitting comfortably in my American life on the other side of the world praying for the Tibetans, idol worship seemed important to attack during intercession. Watching them carve gods out of stone or wood and then bow down to the same statues they had made with their own hands and ask for help as if they held some mystical power seemed not only unconvincing but absolutely foolish. What power could they possibly have now that they didn't have yesterday sitting as a chunk of wood in a forest?

I loved the verses in Psalms, chapter 135, verses 15 -16 that said, "The idols of the nations are silver and gold, the work of human hands. They have mouths but do not speak; they have eyes but do not see; they have ears but do not hear, nor is there any breath in their mouths."

And also Isaiah 44:15-17. "…He makes a god and worships it; he makes it an idol and falls down before it. Half of it he burns in the fire…and the rest of it he makes into a god, his idol, and falls down to it and worships it. He prays to it and says, "Deliver me, for you are my god!"

I loved those verses because it all just seemed so cut and dried. Of course, something you made with your own hands can't save you or help you. I was sure that once I informed these misled people that there was a living god, a real one, not one they had made themselves, how easy it would be for them to let go of their simple beliefs.

It seemed like this was just a lack of knowledge, and I could easily supply them with the missing piece!

Imagine my shock when I was told very kindly and patiently by a Tibetan that the statues themselves were not technically worshipped but that they were just tangible symbols and a re-minder of their greater faith and doctrines…. kind of like a cross.

When I arrived into the lives of those people who had carved out a way of being on the opposite side of the planet from me, their religious beliefs had seemed rudimentary and flimsy at first glance. Once I started learning about the why behind a lot of the Buddhist rites, I could see that this was a profound and well-thought-out philosophy, and it made me grow much-needed respect for those I had come to notify and correct.

I was completely embarrassed by my arrogance and ashamed by my presumptuousness. As I got to know the people who practiced Buddhism, I saw how smart they were, and I'm horrified to admit that I must have somehow inwardly assumed otherwise.

Very slowly, I started to comprehend more of Buddhism's teachings closer to how they were meant to be understood.

When I initially read that Buddhists believe the world and all that is in it is an illusion, I gawked in ridicule that objects you can touch with your hands would be deemed a figment of my imagination.

But I had missed the entire point of the teaching, which is that "things we see in the world are not real not because they don't exist…but because they are mere by-products of our senses. Just as color blindness causes some people to not distinguish certain colors, our senses cause us to see the world one way, which is not the 'true' way." (https://www.buddhabodhi.org/world-of-illusion.html.)

"Very clearly, the external world exists in the real sense of the word. However, when the external world impinges on our senses, we react by projecting ideas, values, assumptions, and expectations onto it. As a result, what we perceive is often more

a product of our minds than the qualities of the object itself."
(http://www.buddhisma2z.com)

"A very simple to understand example is money. Money today has no intrinsic value other than the value we put in it as a
means of transaction. If you were stranded on a deserted island,
would you rather have $1,000,000 or a fishing pole?" (https://
www.buddhabodhi.org/world-of-illusion.html.)

Okay. So things were not as simple as I thought.

There was a rhyme and reason for all of the things they did
that made sense, and there was no way for me to disregard their
way of belief as nonsense.

Because it wasn't.

It definitely wasn't.

It also caused me to re-examine a lot of the things I had just
accepted in my own religion without bothering or making an
effort or taking the time to take a closer look.

I began to strive to find the behind-the-scene information in
the Bible as I read the words on the pages. I sought to find the
why and the heart and the context behind memorized passages
singled out for their encouragement or call to action.

My view and perspective broadened, and I started stripping
away some of the cultural influence that I had unknowingly
strapped onto my own doctrines and beliefs.

This made my faith stronger and my respect for the Tibetan
people greater. Win-win.

But watching Buddhists perform difficult or time-consum-
ing rituals to rid themselves of previous wrongdoing continued
to be hard for me. I was concerned that they were wasting the

precious time they had left on this earth. It was heartbreaking for me to watch prostrators making their way hundreds of miles along the dusty roads to get to holy sites, splaying themselves out on the muddy roads just to get up and do it all over again. Seeing prayer wheels spun round and round and home altars meticulously cared for and new prayer flags strung up on the rooftops felt worrisome. Because, at my core, I didn't think these practices were getting them closer to the outcome they desired.

Their eternal fate seemed to hang in the balance before my very eyes, and I felt the weight of this job crushing my shoulders. While their way of explaining the world around them seemed plausible and many of their rituals seemed to work towards similar things that I worked toward in my personal spiritual faith and practice, it lacked one thing. And that one thing felt big. Huge. Massive.

Catastrophic if it was absent.

That one thing missing was Jesus, and it seemed up to me to make the introduction. When I looked around, I was the only one there who had met Him.

I wanted to connect Grandfather and his wife and a million more to the God who became man and left heaven to come to this earth as a baby, living a human life, so that He could understand suffering just as we do. I wanted to show them the hope and freedom I had experienced in accepting the righteousness He offered to give to me that He had gained by choosing to die even though He had never sinned.

Our goals were similar. Restoration and peace and escape from our current predicament. Our problems were the same:

suffering and sin and death and misery. Our solution was different.

But I lacked the words I needed to speak in their language to say that I had been washed clean by no merit of my own, and Jesus was standing here with us, ready to love and restore and fill with peace and hope.

Were they ready to hear those words? How would they respond? Where would we go from there?

While I pondered how long it might take me to learn the vocabulary for all that I hoped to convey to these precious souls, God was busy making sure the wait wouldn't be as long as I was expecting.

One morning, I was washing my clothes in a tiny river that snaked its way alongside the main dirt road leading to Nangla village. A car came speeding by, and I thought I heard someone yelling my name, and then the car came to a quick stop. What a strange coincidence that another foreign worker I knew from the city was just passing through this section of this vast prefecture. It was too perfectly timed to be accidental. She ended up spending the night with me in the home of Grandfather and his wife, Grandmother, and the other family members.

With more language under her belt, my co-worker used pictures to tell the story of the God-above-all-gods who made the world and everything in it and who had a plan to conquer sin and death once and for all through His Son Jesus.

At the end of the book, Grandmother smiled and said, "I believe, I believe."

Was it really so simple?

Then why was she up bright and early the next day, pouring water into the silver bowls on the altar and using her beads to chant her Buddhist prayers? Was she adding Jesus to the mix of what she already knew about the spiritual realm, happy to add one more helper? Or was she being polite, saying what she thought she was supposed to say?

If someone were to believe in Jesus, how *would* they renounce their old faith? Which rituals could stay and which would need to go? How much culture could remain, and which parts of their identity would need to be shed? These questions weren't things I knew to ask before I watched it unfold before my eyes.

No, this was definitely not straightforward.

There was no time to waste; early the next morning, we began a two-hour hike up the mountain. Reaching the top, we began a 6-hour search on hands and knees among the thorns and weeds for the tiny but coveted "summer-grass winter-worms." Minutes of silence would pass, and then someone would scream, "buh!!!!!!!", the Tibetan word for this creature. Everyone promptly jumped up with cheers and whoops to watch the unveiling of the found treasure.

"Buh" "forms when a parasitic fungus hijacks and devours the bodies of ghost moth larvae that have burrowed into the alpine soil for up to five years. It then steers their bodies to the surface so it can spread its spores (treehousegude.net)."

It is sold as medicine - sixty-two cents apiece, which feels significant when you live as a subsistence farmer and these insect plants are literally in your back yard. Its sellers boast that it can cure cancer and stop aging, among plenty of other things.

But, like most things in Tibet land, searching for "buh" is probably more about the community spirit and camaraderie of the hunt and just being together than the actual monetary value.

It is totally like fishing. Nighttime brings stories of "the big catch." The joy of finding the "buh" is re-lived amongst the neighbors, and the prized find is shown to all.

Four hours had passed, and still, I had found nothing. Grandfather and Grandmother also had seen nothing, but their teenage son had been on a roll. I was growing antsy, impatient, tired, and hungry. My eyes felt crisscrossed and blurry, and I wasn't sure if this was fun anymore.

But then I found one. I actually found one. I think it was one of the most gratifying experiences of my life. The joy I experienced seemed ridiculous, but there it was.

I thought about that verse about the angels in heaven rejoicing over one sinner—just one that had been lost, which had now been found. I think I understood just a little bit more. What about this family? This community? Would the angels one day rejoice over them? It was a really, really big question.

CHAPTER 8

*L*ike Kel's village, snugly located in a lush valley at the foot of the mountains, there were hundreds more, and I discovered many others over time. Often it was because I had met someone in the city, and they invited me home with them, just as Kel had done.

Sometimes, I just happened to stumble into a special place.

Laga is one of those special places. Its breathtaking beauty is enough to capture anyone's heart, but the rich assortment of lifestyles it hosts is a tourist's paradise. Monasteries, nunneries, nomad camps, and a quaint stretch of town begged me to get off the bus when it screeched to a halt, setting off plumes of dust that clouded one's vision for a few minutes.

I didn't need to worry about finding accommodations because so many plump and friendly Tibetan women were there not only to tell me how great their little home turned hotel was, but were quite strong at grabbing hold of my elbow and moving forward quickly. My feet tripped behind me as I tried to handle my loaded backpack hanging and bouncing only over one shoulder, as I wasn't afforded the time I needed to secure it properly.

That was how I ended up sleeping in a room with multiple, sword-wielding men wearing oversized aviator sunglasses and their petite wives with massive coral and turquoise pieces looped through their long hair. The room had a yak skull over the living room door, and I was guided to sit next to a large yak stomach filled with rancid-smelling yak butter, which would imminently be offered to me for consumption. I opted instead for the very wet, stringy-looking cheese, which I was urged to dip in sugar or spice. When it entered my mouth, the strength of the taste filled my entire body, much like the feeling of getting water up your nose in a heavily chlorinated swimming pool. As I tried not to sputter or cough, I reminded myself that offering coffee to these people might spark a similar reaction. It's all about what you are used to.

There was no bathroom, and I found using the yard slightly tricky. I felt exposed during the day or nervous at night, as I couldn't see the animals I could easily hear. I was also aware that I needed to get it right, as I did not have many spare clothes. I had learned that lesson the hard way. I was offered a basin with warm water for washing up in the morning, which felt heavenly in the crisp air.

In the end, my hosts refused payment no matter how much I pushed, and over time many of these small hostel owners turned into very close friends rather than just savvy business entrepreneurs. I wasn't the typical tourist and came back repeatedly, wanting to talk for long hours in their native tongue. We opened up alien worlds for each other, and I believe the benefits of these relationships were mutual.

On my first trip to this town, I decided to hike through the rolling hills to a nunnery in the distance. I could see the thousands of prayer flags dotting the remote mountainside, and the two-hour hike was glorious under blue skies and sunshine. I navigated some angry dogs, not knowing that particular situation was much more serious than I realized at the time, as rabies abounded. Still, I was greeted by a smiling, head-shaven woman in robes at the end of it all.

When I discovered she spoke less Chinese than I did, and my Tibetan was still almost non-existent at that point, I thought our friendship would be finished before it even began. But lo and behold, she took me firmly by the hand and led me into the tiny, one-room dwelling place she called her own. It was made out of blocks of wood, chinked into position like the little homes I had made out of Lincoln Logs as a child.

As we entered her damp, dark home, I immediately felt cold even though the outside temperature was like a perfect fall day. I shivered as I squinted in the darkness and had trouble focusing. The only assistance given was the faint flicker of a butter lamp placed in front of the idols on the solitary shelf. As my eyes adjusted, I could see pictures of gods and goddesses covering the walls in all shapes and sizes.

She guided me to sit on the hard, wooden bed and immediately poured salt tea. An open bucket of homemade butter sat on the well-used table, and I watched as her weathered hands first dug into the mass of yellow and then dropped a large amount into my bowl. The butter immediately began to melt, and she urged me to drink.

It didn't bother her one bit that conversation was next to impossible, and she never seemed to tire of boldly looking at me with her curious, inquisitive eyes. I stared back because, well, what else was I supposed to do?

It felt like being so different from each other somehow inevitably worked to make us instant friends, and she became a regular stop on my travels over the years. There were times I'd make the trek, only to find she was away on a journey. Without the aid of phones, there was no way to make contact ahead of time.

One particular time, I arrived with a special surprise for her. She greeted me with frantic actions to indicate that she had taken both a vow of silence and a vow of fasting from food for the day. Bummer. I set the bags of special food I had ordered as a rare treat for her from one of the few very small Chinese restaurants in the closest town on her old table and sat down.

Not to talk. And not to eat.

So I made myself comfortable and read books beside her and spent the night on her wooden floor so we could wait out the fast and eat, drink, and chat the following day.

I hesitate to mention this part, as I know it may sound dramatic, and in no way do I want this to reflect negatively on my amazing and lovely host, but quite a few rats were keeping me company throughout the night. This was just part of life out here, there was no way around it, and to those who lived here, it was much like how we felt with a fly in the house. A nuisance, yes. Something to freak out over, no. I will say, I had not nor did not ever get to be comfortable sharing space with these critters. It was a very fitful night if I even slept, and I kept the sleeping bag I had brought entirely pulled over my head.

For your sake, I have kept my rat stories to a minimum, as they could easily feature every other chapter. Once I woke up an entire household by my screams because a rat had found its way onto my bed, and the whole family awoke to see me standing barefooted in my long underwear. It was a story they loved to tell every time I visited, and the laughter only got louder and more prolonged over the years. It even became the kind of story they found worthy enough to share with guests who visited their home from their village, and those guests also always found my response to this situation hilarious.

In the morning, being able to finally talk with my host, all of the night's misery seemed far away. My regular visits with Sona the nun over the years were a very interesting test of my language skills. Because I met her so early on in my time in China, I watched my progress unfold before her eyes, which helped me measure how things were going during each subsequent trip. She was very patient and encouraging and seemed genuinely delighted at my visits. It felt like we both waited in anticipation of what and how much more we would be able to communicate during our next visit.

I remember the first time I shared with her about my faith, a bit into my years in China. She had been walking around the monastery, its edges lined with shiny prayer wheels the size of a small vehicle, each inscribed with prayers. This was an important ritual and method for those seeking enlightenment, and she paused to ask me about my own beliefs.

I was pleasantly surprised to feel that my limited language worked quite well during this particular conversation. I have at times wondered if there was something supernatural or miraculous about that specific encounter, but I think there is no way to know. Whether or not God Himself put the words in my mouth, or if it was just that she did a good job of sticking in head nods and grunts at pivotal points, I am not sure, but I tried to state that I had faith in Jesus and did my best to tell the story of His birth, life, death, and resurrection so that I could get the two of them at least acquainted. I was desperate to explain His power, uniqueness, and role in saving any and all of humanity who called out, "Save me!"

I said Jesus is good news. For me. For her.

I left some scripture for her, the books of Luke and Acts, as they were only two of five books that had at that point been translated into her written language. I thought that if she hadn't understood my crude gospel explanation, this would help.

She could read about the life, death, and resurrection of Jesus for herself. As a nun, she had been educated and was literate, a novelty in this area of the world.

It was odd to see those books sitting on her makeshift altar, next to the spinning wheel and golden statues, and I wondered how strange or comforting or how foreign or how true the words might feel to her as she read them.

I hoped that as Sona saw me working hard to learn her language, she also would feel the urgency of the message I was working so hard to bring her. That she would see that it was important enough for me to study for and valuable enough for me to labor over learning how to share it in words she could understand.

I also hoped she would conclude that it had been worth the wait.

Village women

CHAPTER 9

I had been on the field for ten months. I was holed up in one of the few less-than-desirable guest houses not too far from Sona's nunnery. I was relentlessly vomiting from food poisoning, and there was only one public outhouse for all of the guests' bathroom needs. There was no running water, and I was miserable.

I remembered the romantic visions that filled my head as I prepared to come overseas. The excitement that bubbled out of me at the mention of this faraway place with exotic people and gorgeous landscapes. The dream that I gripped and clutched and wound around and around my heart and then watched unfold before my eyes. There was just so much to be grateful for.

But at this moment, I just couldn't see it.

As I heaved myself up to vomit again in that tiny guesthouse, I yelled out, "What prize do I get for this?"

The constant reveling in my novel surroundings was becoming much less constant.

The gratifying feeling I had of merely existing in this fascinating location was fading and fading fast.

The experiences that had once felt so dreamlike just weren't hitting the spot like they used to.

And I was concerned when I stared this fact in the face.

And maybe I was slightly discouraged or even angry that things might not be as great as I had initially cracked them up to be.

As I yelled out to God in that small, slightly-unkempt guesthouse room, I asked Him, the One who had offered the ultimate sacrifice by sending His only son into the world to die, what prize piddly little me would receive for puking into a bucket in the middle of nowhere. I thought I deserved something good.

But the biggest concern of all was that what I was really worried about was if I could hack it. Did I really have what it took to endure? And then, even if I could, did I want to?

The things that at first felt purely interesting had, over time, come to be things that ate at my resolve.

Like privacy.

In the beginning, I was so enamored by being included in peoples' every move that not being able to change clothes for a week seemed a minimal price to pay. Privacy did not seem to be a value to the Tibetans as a whole, and their particular lifestyle didn't lend itself to offering it very easily, anyway. As we've covered, they often all slept in the same room, and bathrooms didn't exist or were only holes behind partial walls. Bathing was also a group event. If there were no privacy concerns with these extreme examples, you could imagine there was no privacy in any other common, more-public areas of life.

I was an extrovert and didn't think I needed much alone time. But I found that my limit for staying in other people's homes in this particular fashion was getting shorter and shorter. So obviously, my invisible ceiling was being encroached upon.

The beginning of the straw that would break my camel's back came for me one week at Kel's family home in a moment that was not such a big deal in hindsight, but somehow managed to do me in.

I needed just a minute of not feeling "on." I was starting to feel like I was almost a show and that I had to always keep the conversation going, be interesting, be friendly, and be the tangible hands and feet of Jesus. I was being touched at anyone's whim and would need to answer any manner of personal questions all day long, and I was starting to feel exhausted.

I decided I just needed a quick moment to collect myself. I quietly and carefully climbed my way up the chinked log laid against the house's multiple stories to the rooftop. I was feeling crabby and spent. I asked God for help, for strength, for... well, nothing else, because before I even made it through a full sentence of prayer, I had not only been located but I was being summoned to sing a solo for the entire town who had gathered in the village center and were waiting for me.

I got through it.

I put on a smile, and I sang "Amazing Grace." And for a moment, all was okay again. God's amazing grace was indeed sufficient, and I felt recharged. Something happened in my tired heart as I testified of God's goodness and grace in a language they didn't know, and it seemed as if an uncommon stillness settled in that place that I couldn't ignore. God's presence was with them and with me. I was reminded of all that God could and would do.

I prayed those words over them as I sang, "when we've been there 10,000 years, bright shining as the sun, we've no less days to sing His praise then when we'd first begun," and felt sure that these people could know His power and this amazing grace personally.

I was in awe that I got to be a part of it all. I was back in the game. It was a redemptive moment.

But it was short-lived.

I didn't like seeing lice crawling through the hair of the people I was staying with. I got annoyed that I had to find the police station and report every single place I visited to the local authorities. I was short-tempered when people who said they were going to show up didn't show up and when people who never told me they were coming were suddenly there, expecting me to drop everything for hours on end.

I was flat-out angry when I specifically sought out a shower by negotiating a price for a hotel room in a very rudimentary and uncared-for building. I double-checked that the room did indeed come with a shower, demanding to see it with my own eyes before putting down my money. Yes, I was losing it.

The owner proudly showed me the shower head located directly over the squat hole in a tiny tiled room. I paid my money and got ready for my weekly shower.

But the owner had neglected to tell me that although they did have a shower, they did not, in fact, have water. After not having water touch my body in over a week, the thought of continuing on that path for several more days felt like too much. And to my embarrassment, I let the hotel owner have a piece of my mind because I felt like he intentionally deceived me, swindling me out of my money and sanity. It is not one of my proudest moments.

More than that, I was starting to get nervous. How would I make it for the long haul if I was struggling with such simple things? What, if anything, could sustain me?

Honestly, at that point, there was some disappointment in understanding that this is what my life would be, which was very surprising, as I was in the middle of the actual fulfillment of my every hope and dream. But there was quite a lot of real discomfort in my life. This was no walk in the park. It was an extremely rustic lifestyle, and it was remarkably taxing to function daily in two excessively-difficult languages. I had to do it almost completely alone, which had considerable struggles. The hardships felt uncompromising and seemed to pile on top of each other.

In that guesthouse, sicker than I may have ever been, I snapped. I lost the mental battle. I lost my way. Or maybe more accurately, I should say, the way before me became crystal clear. And it didn't look pretty. It looked brutal and mean and harsh and uncompromising.

If you study overseas life of any kind, they often refer to the honeymoon phase. That period where everything feels blissful and happy and perfect. And then they say there's almost always a crash.

So. Ah yes.

Here was my crash.

The question was, what would I do about it?

Words from the Bible sprung into my mind and my heart.

"Even after you have done all I have asked of you, you are still an unworthy servant. Yet, I no longer call you servant but friend. Count it a blessing that you should suffer while following the call of the gospel of Christ."

Could I count it a blessing? When I felt like suffering was just part of my daily habits, as familiar as brushing my teeth or making my bed. Could I count it a blessing on the worst days, too? What about when the bad days piled up on each other, and the good days were hard to remember?

I was stinky. I was skinny. There were basins filled with vomit next to my bed. And then the door handle broke off in my hand when I tried to leave the room, and I was literally, actually, stuck with my filth.

When I was well enough, I poured my weak body over the wooden sill and climbed out the second-story window. I shimmied down the makeshift shed, which kept the firewood dry, and made my escape from the locked room. No one had responded to my banging over the previous hours, and I wasn't sure when anyone would be back. I shuffled out to the grasslands to breathe in some much-needed fresh air.

The massive snow mountains exploded out from the lush, rolling green hills, and horses decked in colorful ribbons dotted the pastures filled with wildflowers.

Yes, I was living my dream.

But I wasn't so sure I wanted to be.

I rested my weary head in my hands and cried.

And then.

His sweet Word. "For the joy set before Him, He endured the cross."

He endured.

That's what I needed to hear at that moment because that's all I was doing: enduring. And Jesus had moments like that as well as He followed his call.

Sure, maybe following my call was peanuts compared to the journey Jesus had needed to take, but I knew those words and His example were there for me.

So what was going to hold me here? What would sustain me?

The exotic location and the adventure of the unknown would not be enough, as I was rapidly beginning to realize, nor should it be. The primitiveness of it all was hitting me square in the face, definitely overriding any of the other positive attributes the place boasted at the moment.

And then there were the people themselves. I cared about these people. Their stories had emblazoned themselves onto my heart and soul, and they mattered to me so very much. I liked them. I enjoyed them. They were genuine friends.

I landed specifically on the nomad woman who had arrived at my doorstep and lived with me for three months in the city as she tried to sort through her hurt. I had just visited her in her own home, as she had gone back to reconcile her differences with her husband and mother and be there for her children. Her heartbreak could still be seen in the lines on her face, and her feelings of being unloved and unwanted seemed to strip away any bit of joy left in her.

A friend of mine started singing these words to her as we spent time in her home with the children off at school and her husband out working. "I have a maker. He knows my name. Before even time began, my life was in His hands (Tommy Walker)."

Yes. She has a creator. Who loves her. Who made her. Who had plans and purposes for her that were good. She mattered to God. And she mattered to me.

So what about her? Was she worth it? Was she worth some discomfort on my part to be reached with the good news of Jesus for the first time?

Of course.

And this woman who was so important and so vivid to me was only one tiny little drop in the bucket next to the masses of people located just here, in this one prefecture of Tibet inside the huge country of China inside a great, big old world.

Were they worth it?

Yes. They were worth it.

But hold up.

Would a desire for the people of this place, no matter how lovable or valuable they were, be enough? Enough to hold me here when the going got rough?

I mean, my initial passion and zeal for this lifestyle had begun to fade, so was it possible my passion and zeal for these beautiful people could fade at some point, too? I mean, it was possible they could become even *hard* to love in some situations because, just like me, they might make mistakes sometimes, too.

Passion for people was not going to work.

I settled on the fundamental question being, is Jesus worth it?

Bottom line, this was all about Him, right? It was about His worth, His glory, and His fame.

And yes, He was worth it.

My passion for this place seemed to have disappeared. My passion for these people would probably give out. But my passion for Him? Well, I'm hoping that one won't fade.

And if it does, that probably means I shouldn't be here anyway.

So I threw myself into the clutches of Jesus. I had nothing left of myself and found out that that was a pretty good place to be. I had to rely entirely on Jesus to carry me through, and not myself.

I was thankful for the strength and confidence I had in His call that I felt in my life. It helped to sustain me when I floundered. In that first big crash of my career, I had a choice to make, and in the end, it was a simple one. I chose to obey. I believed that God had asked me to come to this place, and He hadn't asked me to leave. So, instead of packing up my bags and saying I gave it a shot, I said okay. I'm weak. I'm confused. I'm tired and still slightly angry. But, I made up my mind to stay. I decided to move forward, and I went all in.

Maybe too far in, because in the throes of my new resolve, I decided I needed to take another step towards living like the locals and try to lose a bit more of my foreignness. (I will eventually come to realize this is impossible).

I decided to give up my morning cup of instant coffee, whose granules I carried carefully and safely tucked into my backpack. I was convinced that if I stopped drinking coffee, the gospel would go forth.

Oh, if only it were that easy! In full disclosure, I decided that my toilet paper roll must be in a different category, so I pushed that sheepishly into my pack. But, I threw out my coffee and soldiered on. Literally, carrying my pack, after vomiting for twenty-four hours straight, I climbed steep mountains at very high altitudes to reach Father Ogden's nomad village.

Over the years, I will come to learn that nomads speak a completely different dialect of Tibetan than the farmers who live in small towns do. I will learn that the written and the spoken language are also totally different. And that every time you go over a significant mountain pass, the dialect changes again. But for now, I fumbled through with my basic Chinese, as the nomad father, Ogden, fumbled in his basic Chinese.

Instead of chatting, his wife and I bonded over milking the yaks and churning the butter. Their daughter and I collected the jugs for water and skipped out to the stream not too far away to get water for tea, and I marveled at the beauty of this hidden paradise on the rooftop of the world. I taught them how to play a simple card game after a dinner of warm soup.

And then night fell, and there I was, left alone with my too-fresh thoughts. Some of the moments of my day could be classified as purely magical. Here I was, lying inside a nomad tent, under a blue tarp, while the rain gently drummed my entire body. I was alone — alone in the sense that there was no one like me for miles and miles around.

But not alone, because at that moment, I could've reached out and touched Ogden's wife, who was so shy she couldn't even look me straight in the face but also couldn't keep her legitimate smile from stretching ear to ear.

I could've reached out and touched her sweet girl who knew how to care for the baby yaks and who ran barefoot over boulders.

And there was the father himself, a man who had never known anything other than an honest, tough day's work of subsistence living. Baby yaks also stirred within arms reach. I had long yearned to live among this unreached people group. This felt like the embodiment of the whole kit and kaboodle—a rewarding and notable moment.

But I still had that feeling of "Well, this is an unpleasant situation." I never thought that yak hair tents might not be waterproof. Or that the tent floor might actually be nothing more than the muddy ground. Or that there would be feces. Lots of it. Right next to me.

It was amazing. And it was terrible. And I wanted to go home to America. And I never wanted to leave. And I was sure that God wanted me in that place right then. And I couldn't figure out what difference my being there at that moment really made, for the life of me.

I sighed and rolled over.

It was settled.

I was here to stay. Now I just needed to learn how to talk to them.

CHAPTER 10

*M*y desire to get to know Grandfather and Sona the nun and Ogden and his nomad family as much as I could felt urgent and fierce. I wanted to know these people like God knew them. They had things to say, and I wanted to listen to them all, but the sounds their mouths produced didn't seem to land anywhere in my brain. I was itching and scratching to connect more deeply with them, and I was more than willing to fight for it. My formal Tibetan studies were about to begin, and I couldn't have been any more eager and delighted, proven by my inability to sleep the night before classes started.

I was thankful for my year of Mandarin study, and there was some angst at putting my Chinese books back on the shelves after a year of intense effort to learn that language. I'd come a long way and finally felt comfortable navigating the world around me.

Knowing that after all of that, I was headed back to square one to begin to learn a different language felt frustrating, especially when, from what I was told, this new language was even more of a doozy than Chinese. But I was pumped. The Tibetan people had my heart, and the Tibetan language would only unlock more opportunities to connect deeply.

When our teacher arrived, she had just rolled out of bed. I was a bit shocked, but my enthusiasm was not yet dampened. She began to write Tibetan script on the chalkboard, and she didn't stop until every inch of the board was covered.

I wondered what would happen next. She called on one of the eight students to read the message aloud. He stammered in Chinese, "I can't read Tibetan." So she called on another one of us, and in shock, when she realized none of us knew *anything* about the Tibetan language (that is why we are in level 1 Tibetan), she sat down and, in frustrated Chinese, said, "Then I can't teach you."

That first month was much of the same, as we figured out how to help a teacher who had never taught before learn how to teach. My Tibetan slowly improved. And by improved, I mean I started to have very simple conversations, usually with things repeated over and over by both myself and the person I was talking to. Quite a few charades were also probably thrown in.

I could now ask you if you were a monk, a farmer, or a nomad, what crops your hometown produced if your grassland was big, and how many yaks you had.

But the differing dialects were killing me. We had two teachers balancing our class load, and, eventually, we realized they were teaching us two different dialects under the Tibetan language umbrella. It was frustrating to learn something in one class, only to be corrected for saying it an hour later in your next class.

We were encouraged to practice our new skills on the streets, but it only got more complicated as each person seemed to be from another part of the countryside with its own individual, complex way of speaking. To make matters worse, I was still needing to speak Chinese every day as I went to the market, took public transportation, and was just a resident of the People's Republic of China. The languages and dialects got mixed up in my brain, and I felt I couldn't keep them separated or make anything of value come out of my mouth.

My brain was freaking out.

There was no way to get around the challenging task of learning to speak, read, and write Tibetan except directly through it with a lot of hard work. It was slow going, and I missed the relative simplicity of the Chinese language. Such pretty books with systematic approaches to learning a universal language that works wherever you travel in that vast country. But there seemed to be no end to Tibetan dialects, and the books to help you learn some form of this vernacular were extremely few and unexpectedly confusing. The easiest method seemed to be just plugging along day by day, adding vocabulary, and listening intently to try and figure out grammar structures. It was a labor of love; there's no other way to describe it. When communication did happen successfully with people I cared about, the hard-won victory was exceptionally sweet.

The school had agreed to let me study in a Tibetan area for three weeks as part of my program each semester to help me be immersed in the dialect I was currently specializing in.

The village teacher that I had worked so hard to set up ahead of time and whom the school had agreed to count as an extension of their foreign language program didn't materialize once I arrived; something that I would learn was just a part of doing business in this part of the world.

But, the teacher who bailed on me *did* point me in the direction of another teacher. Her name was Teacher Sunshine, and oh, was she sunshine! She was the jackpot of jackpots. She was an excellent teacher - my very first one! She knew how to teach, a natural gifting she had coupled with a solid educational background. She was a science teacher by day and also a mother at heart. She quickly took me under her wing as a student, as a learner of culture, as a younger sister, and as a friend.

She deposited me straight into the teacher dorms at the school where she worked. It was a very small cement room with a mattress-free twin bed covered with several thick blankets for warmth. A piece of plywood provided the structure to lie on. There was a bedpan under the bed, which Teacher Sunshine said I must use after seven p.m. because it was not safe to go out after dark to the outhouse. I was thankful, but not because of the safety concerns, which I didn't see as valid because I considered myself a young and invincible human being. I was thankful because the pile of feces covered in maggots had not been emptied in a long while, and it was currently an above-ground mound you needed to squat over.

There was an electric coil in my dorm with a small tea kettle on which I could heat water. This was my saving grace, as it allowed me to fill my water bottle with hot water and put it in the bed with me to warm my hands and body so I could try to ward off the cold enough to fall asleep. But when the snow came a few days into my stay, the electricity disappeared, which I guess was more than commonplace here, and I lost even that small luxury. My hands were constantly frozen, so much so that I could not even write to take notes during my class sessions with Teacher Sunshine and had to move into purely oral studies.

She came to teach me each day in my tiny room until one day, she started packing up my stuff and announced I would be sleeping at her house so I could meet the rest of her family. I joined in her excitement by asking if I could try to cook them an American meal for supper. I wanted them to like me, and I wanted to earn my keep. We headed to the colorful market to pick out what I needed to make a slightly modified version of spaghetti and red sauce.

It took us 20-30 minutes to walk to her home, weaving through dirt paths and around hills and over makeshift bridges straddling bubbling streams. Her home appeared suddenly just beyond a bend in the road, snuggled against a hillside. We first passed by an extensive and well-taken care of garden that grew potatoes, cabbage, and cilantro, which her family crafted into hand pies and various dishes to be served over rice.

The house's main room was homey, with thick, light-colored wooden beams and a well-swept dirt floor. Fabrics depicting horses and auspicious symbols decorated the room, and paneling blocks were painted with bright colors and intricate designs. Vases of fake flowers brightened the dimly lit space, and all in all, it had a very cozy feel.

The kitchen was more rudimentary, built for function rather

than ascetics, although they had a very impressive bucket and pulley system rigged up for easy water retrieval from down below.

Teacher Sunshine, her husband, her only son, both of her parents, and I ate and drank and made merry for hours. I felt happy to contribute to a unique experience for them of trying some foreign food, something I had the pleasure of doing every single day of my current life.

The next morning, teacher Sunshine's mom was the first to wake. She left her sleeping seven-year-old grandson in the warm, small bed she rose from. She hurriedly placed her thick, sheepskin robe over her long underwear, trying to maintain some of the body heat gained during her long night of sleep. She added thick pieces of coral to her already braided hair and twisted the incredibly long tresses into rings on top of her head. She was ready for the day.

She alone attended to the gods' needs in her home, who they believed protected her and her family. She entered the godroom carrying gifts of food, water, and incense. After offering her humble gifts, I could hear her prostrating herself before the carved, bronze images. As she aged, she found the task getting physically more demanding. When she re-appeared, she grabbed for the red stringed amulet around her neck to make sure it was in place to protect her from any trouble lurking around the corners that she may need to face on this day.

Breakfast preparation had become extremely easy now that the family had an electric blender. After the fire had been started and the water had boiled, the butter tea could be made in just a moment with the push of a button on this new contraption!

She quickly dipped her hand in the butter and rubbed it into her wind-burned face to help protect it against the unforgiving winds of the plateau. She placed the never-ending bowl of barley flour in the middle of the small table and filled up the ancient-looking tea thermoses lined up against one wall, which would provide nourishment for the family throughout the entire day.

Teacher Sunshine was the next to rise, probably awoken by the sound of the blender. Technology does have some disadvantages, but I'm sure she was happy to deal with them in exchange for the excitement TV had brought to their village home. Although Teacher Sunshine had never made it further than 50 miles from her hometown, she could watch images from all over the world, which she chose to do as often as her busy life and working electricity allowed.

She dressed in a robe much like her mother's but much more stylish. She was always very thoughtful in her choice of clothing. The fabric had been brought from Lhasa, the capital city of Tibet. She pulled on her black, high-heeled boots and added a wide-brimmed hat to complete the ensemble. Although she would never wear make-up (she's not that kind of girl!), she took half an hour to apply a seaweed concoction to her face, sold to her by a traveling vendor. He promised her that her wrinkles would vanish, and her skin would become whiter! Teacher Sunshine prided herself on being one of the fashion icons of town, and without trying, I always accidentally thought of her as the Queen of her village.

Teacher Sunshine's dad was still snoring away. He had retired from his job as a police officer and now liked to take things slow. His wife could only wait so long before waking him because it would soon be time to take their grandson to school. Teacher Sunshine's son whimpered as his grandma pulled him out from under the thick blanket. She dressed him as his head nodded and fell – his chin hitting his chest. She babbled a continuous string of encouragements for him to wake up, all to no avail.

She collected his homework and carefully placed it in his backpack. He was given fresh, hot yak milk to drink, and he ate a bit of bread leftover from last night's supper.

Grandpa finally arose, proudly placed his gun in his holster, and donned his police uniform jacket. He may have been done with his official work, but he would always be known and respected as a police officer in this town. The bedding was carefully folded and placed at the foot of the beds because these beds would double as sofas and kitchen chairs throughout the day.

After a quick standard breakfast of roasted barley flour and butter tea (which must be slurped, not sipped!), Teacher Sunshine and I began the walk into town. She stumbled a bit on the muddy path as she made her way through the fields. Could it be the shoes? Walking became much easier on the asphalt when she hit the main road through town. She called out greetings to all those passing by. In this town, everybody knew everybody!

We entered the High School grounds. The music blared distortedly through the speaker system as the students readily participated in the school's mandatory daily exercise program. Many of these children had been chosen as the child in the family with the most academic potential, and if enough money could be gathered, they were sent to live at this boarding school around the age of twelve.

In a few moments, the bell would ring, and every inch of Teacher Sunshine's classroom would be taken up by students eager to learn. A few of her students may go to a second-tier university in the city if their test scores are high enough.

As we went to this school, Teacher Sunshine's parents walked their little grandson to the elementary school in town. Afterward, they gathered on the street with some of the villagers their age to catch up on the activities of others in town. Yes, it was true. Dawa, from just down the road, had purchased a new motor-cycle. A new boss was overseeing the pool tables that lined the streets. And, yes. Two young men had gotten in a fight in front of the noodle restaurant last night.

When they had heard it all two or three times over, they made their way to the religious monuments outside town. After all, they were retired, so they could devote the rest of their lives to earning merit, with the hope of a better life in the next one to come. Sure, most days were the same. Not much changed, but that's just how it was in this little town, and this little town was their pride and joy.

Getting to know this family so intimately made it feel like this place somehow belonged to me in a way. Living in their home and experiencing daily life as just one of the gang was a privilege and a joy. I learned new things about each one of them every day, and they became as comfortable to me as my Aunt Carol or my neighbor Lois back home in small-town America.

I learned in time that Teacher Sunshine's spry mother, who

dresses in ornate traditional clothes each day, does not eat meat. In contrast, Teacher Sunshine's robust, smiley, gun-carrying daddy will eat anything and everything. Almost. A few years later, when he visited my home in the city, I served oatmeal for breakfast, and he kindly but firmly refused to eat what he called "baby food."

Teacher Sunshine's seven-year-old son wanted to know all the English words while I was staying with them, and we had so much fun giggling that I almost got over how I forgot my deodorant on this trip, and that is not something available for purchase out here.

Speaking only this dialect and no English or Chinese for weeks had a surprisingly huge impact on my communication ability and comfort with this language. It felt like exponential growth, and I was not complaining.

I also found that besides watching my vocabulary and fluency grow, I became an accidental detective. I learned that I could catch all kinds of clues through body language and could even often predict where a particular conversation may go, helping me prepare words more quickly in my brain. The more I got to know a person, the more I got to know their particular conversation fillers, like "you know" or "uh." Another helpful thing in deciphering conversation was understanding their personality. Are they a jokester? Are they serious? Do they tend towards certain topics of conversation? Do they repeat stories? Do they ask a lot of questions?

Reluctantly, after my time was up, I headed back to the city to fulfill the rest of my semester's obligations with the university, which, interestingly enough, included leading the entire foreign student population in a country line dance in a packed arena for what they fondly call "sports day." I procured us all cowboy hats with my limited budget from the administration, and we strutted and swayed and danced the Boot Scootin' Boogie in the heart of China to the applause of thousands.

All in a day's work.

The kitchen in a Tibetan home

CHAPTER 11

A test of how well my language skills were progressing was when I needed to straddle both languages simultaneously in significant ways.

At thirty-one years old, Chen was a fiery, beautiful woman. Although her body was deteriorating from illness, her smiling eyes danced on top of her bright red wind-burned cheeks, and her stark, white teeth provided a stunning contrast to her rich, dark skin. She sat bundled up beside her tired and aged mother. The precious mother began to recount the mysterious disease ravaging her daughter, and she specifically broke down over the level of pain the previous night had forced her child to endure. Her love and concern for her daughter were unrestrainedly evident as she referred to the tears that she couldn't hide.

My heart ached for this mother's undeniable love, even as her child was now a grown woman herself. Clutching my hand, the mother also told me of how she herself had thrown up the first time they left their rented room in the city because the sheer number of people had made her dizzy. The loud, cramped streets with their neon signs and street vendors were a far cry from the tents and grasslands they were used to. For the first time in her life, she had left her small village and journeyed the five days needed to grasp for an answer to her daughter's worsening health. She said that there was a hardness in her daughter's belly, and a constant stream of liquid ran from her belly button. The ride to the hospital took its toll on Chen, and it was so frustrating to hear from the medical staff that there was no available bed for her, that there was no waiting list, and that there was no way to know when her turn would come to be seen or treated.

A few days later, after checking in personally every day by physically journeying to the hospital, the offer came to put her in a bed in the hallway lined up with the other desperate patients. We jumped at the chance, even though we knew the situation was even less desirable than what the restrictive hospital rooms had to offer.

It was a beacon of hope. A possibility. One step closer. A doctor to look at her. Enough for the moment. When the logistics were sorted, I pushed my way into the cafeteria in the hospital, where various people were selling food among the teeming sea of people.

In China, the hospital does not provide food for the patients, and the patient's family and friends are responsible for providing for them. I was the family and friend in this situation. Friends and family can also sleep overnight, squeezed onto the tiny twin bed together. There were no additional seats for family members, let alone beds.

The irony that they needed me, a foreign, American, young

twenty-something with limited language skills herself, to navigate communication and culture in their own country is not lost on me.

There was no line in the food hall, just a huge mass of people yelling out what they wanted to order, but I didn't quite know to whom. Somehow, after much time had passed, I found myself pressed firmly against the glass window and got my hands on something that looked edible. I pushed through the endless mass of shouting people and made it to the elevator, only to be swept along by another crowd of people. I could hardly breathe as we made our way up with people pressed against me on all sides. The lady smashed on my right started to chat with me. She announced that she was eighty-four years old, and with that, she took my hand in hers and held on with a surprisingly firm grip. Together we exited on the tenth floor, and I felt satisfied with my accomplishment as the nomad women settled down to eat. Meeting that felt need bolstered me to keep plugging away at my language studies, that something must be clicking.

I had been practicing retelling a couple of Tibetan folk stories as part of my curriculum at school, and I decided to try my luck at being understood by these two women on a more daring subject than lunch.

And so I began,

"A long time ago, Aku Denba was on his way back from Lhasa to his home when he ran into some fellow travelers on the road. In jest, Aku Denba shouted at them to eat poop. Instead of thinking it was funny, the travelers became angry and immediately grabbed Aku Denba and dragged him before the town court. When the

judge asked Aku Denba why he had said such a horrible thing,
Aku Denba said he was only joking and meant nothing by it. The
townspeople all agreed that this was not such a serious offense
but nevertheless should have some sort of penalty. They decided
that Aku Denba needed to stand underneath the toilet hole in
the lower half of the outhouse and let everyone poop on his head.
Aku Denba swore that he would obey the order. However, when
it came time for the people to poop on his head, Aku Denba said,
"I have promised to let everyone poop on my head. But I did not
agree to let anyone pee on my head. So I will hold a spear in my
hand, and if even one drop of pee falls on me, I will poke the butts
of the people with my sword." After he said this, all the people were
frightened, and no one pooped on Aku Denba's head (Tibetan folk
tale, author unknown)."

When the mother fell onto the bed laughing, my heart connected with hers over this small moment of joy amidst many
moments of pain and sadness and fear and thoughts of death.

I pulled out a deck of cards. Rumor had it the older woman
was a card shark. I scolded her about betting money, and with
twinkling eyes, she promised to only play for fun. With no TV
and being completely illiterate, these women would have to figure out how to pass the time.

The diagnosis eventually came back to her illness - severe
tuberculosis. It had been left untreated for far too long, and many
of her insides were destroyed. She needed two or three expensive
operations, and even then, the situation did not look good. One
kidney must be removed, as it was completely non-functioning.
The liquid coming from her belly button was confirmed as urine.

Surgically, a new bladder would have to be made out of her small intestine, but she would never be able to urinate properly again. She would have a bag for the rest of her life, and I sensed the doctor was trying to tell us that might not be too long.

The news obviously shook both the girl and her mother, and the fear of the unknown crept into their hearts and mine. My job was to proclaim that a good God was sovereign over all things, and He was so powerful that nothing could stand in his way. Such good news amid such devastating news.

But I wavered. Could this situation be resolved? A mother stood looking at the child she had carried in her womb. A child she nurtured and loved and fed and clothed. A child she would most likely bury in the months to come. I didn't have words. I don't know if I wanted to have words.

God understands this love. God understands this loss.

God so loved the world that He sent His only Son into the world that whoever believes in Him will not perish but have everlasting life.

A friend and I gave them a battery-operated storytelling machine with 45 hours of stories about nomads who lived thousands of years ago, and the hope and life that can exist when you follow the Great Herdsman.

I prayed that the gospel would provide life for them in a way they had never known. Eternal life that stretched beyond the pain and misery that had been promised to them. I prayed and willed and begged that this would be enough hope for them to hold on to in these moments. And I prayed that my fingers would stay clenched around this hope, too.

Watching this mother and daughter relationship made me think of my own mom. Or maybe I should say it made me think of her more. I constantly thought of my family, and being away from them was a cost I had to count repeatedly, and maybe never more than on Christmas.

My mama always called me her "Christmas girl." There was nothing like waking up at my grandmother's house on Christmas morning when I was growing up. Those were probably my favorite moments of the entire year. The Christmas tree twinkling in the early morning hours, holiday smells wafting from the kitchen, stockings filled with treasures.

Listening to my dad read the Christmas story from the Bible and thinking about Mary giving birth in the stable to Baby Jesus warmed every inch of my soul. Even crawling half-asleep into a freezing cold car to go home felt like a magical part of the whole experience. Yes, my mama was right. I was definitely a Christmas girl.

Spending Christmas on the other side of the world was very different from what I had experienced growing up. For the most part, it was beautifully simple and incredibly meaningful. But there was also a whole lot of loneliness.

And I guess that's the first thing to get out of the way when we're talking about Christmas overseas. It's lonely.

Loneliness is an issue most global workers face almost daily. But on Christmas, it just hurts more. And, to be honest, it's just part of the deal. When we left family and friends, comforts, and our favorite snacks, Christmas — as we knew it — was gone forever, too.

Most of us wouldn't trade it. In our minds and deep down in our hearts, we know that. His love compels us to be exactly where we are. And we want to be exactly where we are. I mean, we get to celebrate the incarnation of Christ every single day by speaking the good news of a baby that was born to change everything. How's that for year-round Christmas joy?

But that doesn't mean we don't have moments when we yearn to be surrounded by buttery Christmas cookies and crackling fires and hot chocolate.

When I was overseas, I missed everything about Christmas. I missed the lights, the music, and even the feeling you get when you walk into a church for the Christmas service with everyone dressed in red and smiling while someone plays familiar carols on the piano.

The traditions we left behind, no matter how non-essential, are genuine losses, just like giving up indoor heat or your heart language or your mom and dad.

It's a real sacrifice. It's a real cost.

I learned to take it as a loss, call it what it was, and then accept it. And then slowly, embrace it.

As an extrovert at heart, being alone would not cut it. Without family nearby, I had to get myself some fill-ins. I invited neighbors, friends, and anyone around to come for Christmas brunch, games, and the Christmas story. It was a reminder and a picture of Christ calling all from the highways and byways to His feast.

I got to share some of my favorite traditions and watch

friends' joy unfold as they discovered for the first time the things I had loved for so long. I laughed at neighbors playing games that required them to try unwrapping presents while wearing bulky mittens. I howled as a teacher tried to act out "yak" in a game of charades. I was amazed as I watched guests spend over an hour decorating the perfect Christmas cookie. Experiencing old traditions in new ways brought a different kind of joy.

The forced simplicity of Christmas overseas made everything that much more meaningful for me. I will never forget the years of worshiping Jesus together on Christmas with just a handful of people who represented multiple countries. What a foretaste of glory divine!

Making new traditions became a helpful way for me to bring new joy and significance to the holiday season. I got myself my very own "Charlie Brown Christmas tree." It was as simple as a plant from the local market one year. I began to add my own homemade ornaments year after year to commemorate special events that had happened during the year.

This was pure bliss to my sentimental core and satisfied my constant desire to record and analyze the happenings of my journey. It was a reflective and praise-giving activity to thank God for His sovereignty. By the way, I am not crafty. I cut out photographs, made holes with pens, and tied the thread to each one.

I made a Christmas-countdown paper chain with different names for Christ quoted in the Bible for each day of Advent.

I made new food traditions by force. Not having traditional Christmas foods can be a big letdown. So I started a new custom of having a Christmas Eve "snack meal" by making fun, particular foods that felt familiar but could be made from local ingredients. I made meatballs. I made homemade nachos, first making dough, then cooking tortillas, then frying the triangles. I splurged on dried fruits and nuts that I didn't usually purchase during the year.

I would do a special activity out of the ordinary reserved for the holiday season. For me, that was putting together a jigsaw puzzle each Christmas. This took some forethought, as I purchased a few of them when I was on home assignments to have them ready for Christmas.

On Christmas, we blasted all of the electric space and wall heaters. After being so cold for so long, I ignored the cultural norms and the bill and was warm! Well, warmer, at least.

I learned to celebrate the "family" God provided for me overseas.

We'd gather together and just be. We'd play games, laugh, and talk about our family traditions at home.

And, of course, we'd participate in the blow-up bat bonking tradition that was alive and well all over the streets of China. You may be unfamiliar with this tradition, which of course you are, because WHAT in the world?

It is precisely what I just said. You take inflatable bats and hit as many strangers over the head with them as you can. Americans got hit more than anyone because they all believed that it was our tradition, to begin with.

And then, one day, things got less lonely.

A boyfriend entered the scene.

CHAPTER 12

*I*t all got kicked up a notch and swirled around because of those beloved rats I have mentioned. Two very large and stubborn rats had moved into my very small apartment.

I baked two chicken breasts in my convection oven, which sat on top of my very small countertop. I took them out to cool and left the room.

When I came back, there was only one chicken breast in the pan.

As I stood there trying to absorb the situation, which was so odd that it didn't make any sense in those initial moments, I saw movement out of the corner of my eye. There was a huge furry creature streaking across my kitchen and into a hole under the sink.

So big, my first thought was a cat.

And then, I freaked. Like heart pounding, chest constricting, paralyzed body, extreme shaking, freaked. Rat, rat, rat, rat, rat.

When my body agreed to move again, I tiptoed from the kitchen and then bolted through the living room and into the bedroom, where I slammed the door and jumped onto the bed. Before I could stop trembling, another flash of fur dashed across the room and burrowed under the bed. The bed on which I was currently sitting.

I began to sweat and breathe heavily. I tried to bolster my courage and remember my resolve to do any and all things for Jesus.

And then I called Ethan, the only guy close enough to get to me quickly. And quickly mattered.

I didn't want to call him. I tried to avoid him at all costs in my regular life. Because after the initial months of not really getting him (the pizza and movie guy), I actually got to know him.

I started to understand his choices. To respect his choices. I began to look up to him and even take his advice. I had seen his love for God and his love for people. I saw his heart. And it was considerably beautiful.

He was reserved but wise. He was studious, putting in 40 hours a week of language study while balancing other duties and roles. He embraced the culture full-on, setting his comfort zone aside for the sake of the gospel. While I had been concerned at the beginning about his desire to lock the door and eat pizza, I quickly learned that he spent every Friday and Saturday night participating in traditional Tibetan dancing because that is how the young Tibetan men his age spent *their* free time.

During breaks from study, you could find him chatting and playing on the university basketball courts. First, making small talk and then more profound dialogue with Tibetan students. This often led to meals together, which slowly turned into a deep and meaningful relationship over time. He put in the time and effort to become all things to all people. And I had noticed. Maybe more than I should have.

Concern set in when I realized I also enjoyed spending time with him in social situations. These occasions were generally few and far between, but he was easier to talk to than I had first experienced, and he was funny. I was worried because I knew all of these things added up to a winning combination. And if he didn't feel the same way about me, things could get messy. And, as far as I could tell, he had no interest in me. And so, my solution was to avoid him as much as possible and try to keep him out of my mind.

But rats are desperate times. And desperate times call for desperate measures. A strong, brave, handsome hero. So, I called. Proving my point about his seeming non-interest in me as a girl, he did not come to rescue me. Instead, he told me to go and buy sticky paper and set it out to trap the rats. Then, he said, they would just need to be disposed of once that was done. As he talked me through the actions of what I was supposed to do, I bit my tongue and resisted telling him that all of these steps were actually what I was calling on *him* to do. Not me. That was the point of the phone call.

Time to pull up my bootstraps, I guessed.

Graciously, the bedroom rat soon decided to join the kitchen rat, and I shut the door and shoved a towel underneath the crack, as I had heard rats could squeeze into extremely tight places. I wasn't taking any chances. Sticky traps had been placed, and a night of no sleep fell upon me.

At one point, there was a lot of noise. Squealing. There was much squealing that sounded like it could have been a pig, but it was coming from my kitchen, too close to where I was hunkered down. In time, the noise stopped.

In the morning, I ever so slowly slid open the kitchen door. There were shreds of cardboard everywhere, and a tiny island of what was left of the sticky trap sat telling me the story as it was filled with rat hair. No rat.

I called my knight in shining armor again because these desperate times were just getting more desperate. He advised me to put something heavy over the top of the rat when the squealing began because the squealing was my lovely signal that a rat was caught. He said if I couldn't handle the disposal part, he could come in the morning and take care of it for me. Progress. But I would still have to face the creature head-on in this scenario. Very head-on.

It didn't take long to catch it again, and some of the most nerve-wracking moments of my life involved putting a box over a gigantic flailing rat and topping it with a large jug of laundry soap. The second rat was soon to follow.

And then he came. He took the rats out of my apartment, and I may have cried with relief.

People often ask if there was a spark right away when Ethan and I met. Nope. We were just too different even to begin to want to understand each other. In time, we were forced to get to what mattered by working in an intense environment together. It was obvious we worked well together. And then we acknowledged that we enjoyed spending time together by slowly spending slivers of moments together by choice, but not enough for either of us to know if they meant anything.

When two years had passed, and Ethan had not given me any indication that his feelings went beyond friendship, I let my interest go as much as I could, which wasn't all that hard to do in a fast-paced life full of constant and major distractions.

So I was shocked and baffled when it all came to a head; and we were staring each other down in my living room shortly after the rat incident, and he point-blank asked me to think about marrying him.

The thing is, I didn't have any thinking to do. There were no questions that needed to be answered for me. I knew that to stop loving him would be impossible once I started. And I knew all I needed was permission to start.

It was easy to fold Ethan into my life and for him to fold me into his. The change was small and big all at the same time. We didn't need to get to know each other; we had accomplished that long ago.

Just a few months after we started dating, in a crazy whirlwind of unexpected circumstances, I found myself flying to America almost overnight for Ethan to have a quick but necessary medical procedure. After his recovery, we were ice skating on a pond surrounded by twinkling white Christmas light-laden trees when he presented me with a diamond ring and asked me to marry him.

Of course, I said yes.

We were officially engaged.

Back in China, my days rolled together with just snatches of sleep between them. I was considered a full-time student at the university. I taught English at night through Bible stories in partnership with Chinese believers who wanted to reach Tibetans with the gospel. We had to move location multiple times as tensions mounted between the government and its people, and rioting began all over the province. People were setting themselves on fire in protest—many people. Armed military troops patrolled the streets, and we began to have to show our passports just to enter the gates of our homes.

I began an intense study to learn the Tibetan vocabulary I needed to bring to life the history of the God-above-all-gods and His plan to redeem humanity through His son Jesus. I organized a class to study Tibetan music and discuss how to use it to share the mystery of God becoming man.

I had a revolving door of crises entering my apartment from the surrounding mountain villages. The sick and hurting had learned that God's love in my heart was there for them, too.

I was researching the needs and wants of Tibetan nomads and farmers and trying to plan how I could play a role in bettering both their physical and spiritual lives.

I had found my rhythm. I had hit my stride. And on top of it all, I had fallen in love.

And then, to top it all off, one day, I realized that my Chinese neighbors weren't Chinese neighbors anymore. They were just neighbors. I borrowed cooking ingredients from them, and they watered my plants when I was away on trips, and I took them baked bread, and we chatted and drank tea.

Nomads and farmers and nuns and monks were no longer

strange labels to me but words used to describe people with whom I'd shared both joy and sorrow.

Chinese Christians were not novelties anymore, something to inspect or hoard, but true friends I stayed up with until the early hours of the morning catching up. They were not a project for me. And I was not a project for them. We were sisters. No more. No less.

Jun had moved out and on and had a husband and a beautiful baby girl. I watched her transform from a quiet teenager to a wife and mother.

Kel had left the country with no way for me to contact her. She had been my rock, and now she was gone. As much as I missed her, I knew I didn't need her anymore in the way I used to. We were moving on, spreading our wings and flying, each one of us to whatever lay ahead.

Sona the nun had started teaching at the local nunnery and was studying medicine to be able to help others. I was so proud of her and could see her pride in herself.

And Teacher Sunshine was building a new home with a desire to bring more people from the outside world in and create a place for us to lay our heads when our travels brought us to her village. Her generosity was stunning, and I loved that more of the world would get to experience her zest for life.

Ethan had moved from stranger to teammate to friend to the one I loved.

So many people had entered my life in significant ways since I had set foot in China. Upon arrival, I hadn't known a single one of them. Now their stories and hopes and dreams and losses and pains were divots in my heart, a point of connection that locked us together. Some had come and gone, but their marks were forever embedded into my being. Others were still there, by my side, our stories stretching together into the future.

And I realized that China had ceased to be that foreign land that God had called me to and had become part of who I was. Part of my identity. My stomping grounds.

And then the unthinkable happened.

CHAPTER 13

I hired a tailor to make my American-style wedding dress based on a photo I found on the internet. I knew this was a bit of a risk, but I wasn't sure exactly how else to pull off my upcoming nuptials. I headed into the city center for the first official unveiling and the fitting. I would be leaving China in three weeks to fly back to America to wear this dress in my marriage ceremony, so I was counting on everything coming together smoothly. Little did I know what was coming.

I entered a twelve-story building and climbed to the third floor. The tailor helped me into the heavy gown, and I looked in the mirror at what I would wear the day my life started its next chapter. She took a photo for me to send to my mom when suddenly, everything started falling off the high shelves in the room. There was a terrible rushing noise, like a train, and then the screaming began—an entire building filled with people screaming.

My initial thought was that the building was collapsing. How I didn't know, but as we heard shouts of "run!", we ran. People tripping, pushing, running down stairs. The train of my wedding dress made me an easy victim as people pushed to get past the flowing material taking up space. When we stumbled out into the open air and blue skies, "I'm alive" was all I thought.

The streets were filled with people—a sea of Chinese faces. And a white-skinned girl in a white American wedding dress. But we were safe. We had made it.

But I was still so unsteady. And then I realized that the ground was rolling under me. I heard a sound like an explosion and looked up to see glass windows shattering and water pouring out of the building above me. And I realized we weren't safe. And so I clung to my Chinese tailor. And she clung to me. And I begged her to pray with me, and she begged me to pray because we were scared.

And then it stopped. As quickly as it had begun, it stopped. As people tried to wrap their heads around what had happened, leaders emerged from the masses, making plans for those of us who were in shock. They herded us to an open field, as open as you can find in the middle of a massive Chinese city, and warned us of aftershocks that would likely come in the wake of the earthquake.

For the first time during my life in China, people left me alone. I must have stood out. Barefoot in a dirt patch in what was supposed to be my wedding dress. But life was too precious at that moment. Curiosity was left untouched as people clung to loved ones or tried in vain to reach others on the phone.

I looked over at a girl wrapped in nothing but a towel. So, um, yes, I guess things could have been worse.

Slowly, people started to move. Trying to get home. Wanting to check the damage. Hopefully meet up with loved ones who were unreachable.

We tentatively re-entered the building after watching many others go before us. A quick snatch-and-grab to get purses, hoping that they could get us home, and a wild stripping of the wedding dress.

I couldn't get on any public transportation. I saw few buses moving, and those that were had people stuffed so full that there was no way someone could grab a hand and swing from the outside any more than they already were.

So I began to walk. I was not 100% sure of the way home, but I thought I knew the general direction and would eventually find my way after seeing a familiar landmark. It took miles and hours, but I did finally stumble my way in flip-flops to Ethan's house, which was such a relief to see him living and breathing after not reaching him by phone, as most of the lines were down.

We went to my apartment to check the damage, but we couldn't get in. The door was warped shut. I joined the large group that was accumulating in Ethan's small, first-floor, minimally damaged apartment to wait out the night and try to figure out what next steps should be taken.

The news spewed out horrible things that night on the TV. Dead. Dead. Dead.

People buried. Entire towns flattened. A whole school full of children lying underneath the rubble. Would they get to them in time? I cried for those babies. For those mamas screaming into the night with no home to envelope them in a moment of privacy as they grieved.

And I was terrified, sure the building we were in would topple down on top of me while I slept.

Fear was contagious. The people in our neighborhood spilled out into the streets. Thousands. Into every open space to sleep outdoors. The aftershocks continued throughout the night and the next day and the next.

The visible damage in the city was minor compared to what we saw on TV, 50 miles away from the epicenter of the 7.9 quake. Cracks, broken windows, only a handful of collapsed buildings. The news said that we'd lost 1200 lives in our city. It seemed like nothing when the death toll continued to climb past 75,000 in the areas where building quality was not so good. 4.8 million left homeless.

All of the water had been turned off in the city. We had been told all of the water had been contaminated. Mass hysteria ensued. The stores were emptied of bottled water by panic.

People were getting organized to help. I was ready to go. To hand out water. Blankets. But then they said we'd be pulling out bodies. Some alive. Some dead. I couldn't do it. And I felt like a miserable human being.

I joined a group heading to the local hospitals instead. There were children there who had lost their parents. Their caregivers needed relief, we were told. I could hold babies. Sing to them. Whisper God's promises over them and ask God to give me the faith to believe they were true.

But when I got there, I felt like I was invading their pain.

They were older than we had been told. Teenagers. I felt like my presence signified that they had become a spectacle. A tragic spectacle. Why would they want my comfort? They needed so much more than I could give them on this day. I didn't want them to feel that I was there to gawk at the horror they were living through. I didn't want to add to their grief. I wanted to run. But I stayed. I cried, and I held their hands. The broken bones and gashes pretended to be invisible as they sat next to the wails of loss.

Ethan was able to deliver supplies, and while he was gone, another aftershock ripped the awning off of the building I was in. Hundreds of us fell into the streets screaming. We tried to laugh off our jumpiness and continue with our business. We had become one through this horrific event.

I came to be sure that something was not right with me. I couldn't function, and I was terrified, but everyone else was in a similar situation.

At night I closed my eyes and saw the images from the live coverage on TV - where people took their final breath, right as you watched. I replayed the stories told by the men who had gone to the disaster area and saw the injured faces of the children left without parents that I had seen in the hospital. I dreamed of earthquakes and continued to wake to aftershocks with my heart pounding.

Then one night, another 6.1 earthquake that lasted for forty-five seconds entered my bedroom and left me awake for two hours. I packed a bag to be ready to go but settled down enough to remain in my home. I felt like I couldn't go, but I also couldn't stay. Nowhere felt safe. Nowhere felt right.

Life had changed dramatically in an instant.

Ethan said it was as though one life had finished, and another was starting. Right then, everyone's only concern was physical life. No one cared about work, school, or play. Everything so important last week was now gone from all of our minds. We went from one thing to the next but never knew what that next thing would be. A call for blankets - okay. Gather to pray. Need blood. Okay. No, now they have more blood than they need. Go home. There was no schedule, no planning, no hoping for a brighter future; there was only now.

God is our rock, the other foreign workers said.

But I had trouble reading the word and praying. I felt ashamed because this felt like the time for which I was meant to be here, to offer God's love and care to those who were lost and hurting. But I felt so lost and so hurting. And I felt guilty because my loss and my hurt felt so small next to so many.

When I tried to open my Bible, I read, "Sing a new song unto the Lord." In my heart, I said, "I don't want to sing a new song, and I don't want to sing an old song. I don't want to sing." For the next two days, I didn't open my Bible at all. There was a hardness in my heart. Anger over the massive loss of life, most of whom did not know God, and many, many who probably had never even heard the name of Jesus. I was confused. Why couldn't they have a fighting chance?

We had a debriefing meeting with our organization and talked about dealing with trauma. They said that laughter and everyday things are good. I felt angry that they even suggested that while so many were clinging to life, waiting to be rescued. I was mad if people talked about trivial things. I didn't want to play a game or chat.

And then the day came when they said that any who were still trapped would have died by now. Somehow there was finality in that. The wait was over. Now we took a breath. I gathered with other believers, and we sang a children's song, "My God is a great big God. My God is a great big God. My God is a great big God, and He holds us in His hands." As I watched the life in the children's eyes and thought about how He had watched out for them, I felt grateful. A feeling I hadn't felt in what seemed like too long. There was a softening in my heart, and I could breathe. I could breathe.

They said we must get back to living. But I didn't want to leave the dead behind. I felt like we needed to stay there with them so that they were not forgotten.

It could have been me. Maybe it should have been me.

And oh, yeah. I was supposed to get married in three weeks.

A celebration. Amid the stench of death. It felt impossible and wrong, and I didn't even know if I could do it.

So I left the wedding planning for yet another day, even though the days were shrinking away and the guests were making plans to join us on the other side of the world while we all wear fancy clothes and eat fancy food surrounded by fancy flowers.

I went on a relief trip. Now that the body toll had been calculated and the bodies had been tended to, I signed up to take tarps to a village that had been destroyed. Not a single house was left standing. Tents had all been purchased, and the shelves cleared days before, so tarps would have to do. The gyms all over the city were filled with the homeless, but the villages didn't have the luxury of any remaining structures still standing.

When we arrived, I was struck by the people just sitting on top of the rubble that had been their home. All of them. That was the norm. They just sat—nothing to do. Nowhere to go. A hollow look in their eyes. We didn't have enough tarps to go around, so we were charged with assessing who was most in need of shelter and supplying them with help while their neighbor wasn't deemed destitute enough. They were all more than destitute. What a miserable job. Judging pain and loss and giving it a value.

Again, I felt like a strange pawn in a ridiculous game. How could I really be helping?

It's such a weird thing to want to help so badly but feel like you're just getting in the way. They told me my foreign face would bring the people hope that the world cared about them, and I overheard our leader telling the people that I had come from America to help, even though he knew I had come from just down the road the same as him. Is there hope in lies?

A woman sat over an open fire, heating water in a pot and pouring it into a container of ramen noodles the aid truck had brought. One man had a tarp and laid under it, unmoving but awake. He did not stir as we approached; he did not look our way, wanting to be alone in his grief and loss.

We were taken to a school lying completely in ruins, and I

could not bear to know if the kids had made it out safely or if they didn't. Where were those children now? I didn't ask.

On the way home, we passed less damaged areas. The second story of a building was ripped off while the first story remained. A closet with a few clothes dangling off hangers at weird angles blew in the breeze in what used to be the upstairs bedroom. Cars crushed by boulders. And people. Everywhere people. People whose lives would never be the same.

I walked home in the dark. I opened a suitcase and began to pack. The guilt was suffocating. I was leaving this world behind. This world where I could not walk down the sidewalks near my home because the tarp shanty towns still filled every inch of space. This world where kids would fall asleep without mothers, and mothers would fall asleep with aching breasts full of milk and no baby to drink. This world where homes were no longer homes and lives no longer feel like lives. I walked out with a white dress scrubbed clean of trample marks and rips mended stuffed into my suitcase. And I thought of all of those hearts whose tears will never be mended.

Now we start life again.

CHAPTER 14

*W*e re-entered China six months later as Mr. and Mrs. Wyss. In our short time away, China had magically transformed back into the place we knew. The after-effects of the earthquake were spotted or felt only occasionally for those of us who had not suffered the loss of family or homes.

Those moments generally came in surprising places, like when sitting in a dentist's chair, wiggling ever so gently, and your mind begins screaming for you to run before reality resumes control and lets you know you are not in an earthquake after all. The trauma would fade over time, but I suspect there will always be a corner of my heart taken up by what occurred and our proximity to the horror. I can only imagine the space taken up in the hearts of those who experienced great loss.

The expressionless immigration officer at the Chinese airport didn't speak to me as she took my passport. She stamped it, handed it over the tall counter, and called for the next in line.

"Excuse me," I said, "I don't understand how this visa works." She had given me a tourist visa, but not the typical thirty or sixty-day one that I was used to receiving. Generally, I was required to switch to a different visa to remain in the country by either procuring an invitation from a University or by obtaining appropriate and sanctioned work. This always involved further trips to the immigration center in town with additional paperwork to prove your legitimacy and hope you were granted your request by whoever happened to be working that day.

But this new visa said one year.

"It means you can travel and stay anywhere in China for the next year." I felt frozen to the spot. Was it that easy?

Our previous visas had never allowed us to live permanently in the countryside. We had dreamed of living in a quiet, modest Tibetan village. We had imagined ourselves cuddled up in a small corner of the mountainside that we could call our own but could also share openly and freely with our Tibetan neighbors.

I had invested in some silk long underwear back in the States, and I had already figured out that down coats were worth every penny. I was ready for this. I felt like the cold was my most prominent opponent, and I would not let that stop me. I could so do this.

I couldn't imagine anything better—my little piece of happiness on the Tibetan plateau. After so many restrictions on so many things, this newfound freedom to just BE felt like heaven. Our previous visas had all been tied to a task requiring full-time student status or employment, gluing us to the big bustling city, with trips out to the Tibetan mountainside snuck in whenever we could make it happen in between other duties and responsibilities. Could we flip that on its head? Reverse it?

A very uninterested and unengaged stranger handed us our golden ticket in one thoughtless action.

I packed two pairs of pants, a skirt, three sweaters, a fleece, a down coat, and my silk long underwear for my wardrobe in my new town. We packed a suitcase of Tibetan language study materials, books, and a few games. Tibet is definitely a bring-your-own entertainment kind of place.

The trip out to Jangka, the village we landed on as our home sweet home, is breathtakingly beautiful and shockingly harrowing. When you traverse the sky-high mountain passes on rough roads carved through the stone, it's hard to remember that you are not the last person on the face of the earth.

Its stark and jagged peaks are inhospitable. Winds whip at uncomfortable speeds, and it's hard to catch your breath. Prayer flags scream from the pressure of the icy gales on top of shrines made by human hands, and rocks are piled on top of each other as offerings to the gods in search of safety on such a dangerous journey as this. Descending into the valleys, you can often see yaks sprinkled across the mountainsides, but usually no herder is in sight. A solitary farmer's home, made of stones stacked on top of each other, makes its way into the landscape every great once in a while.

And then, it seems to appear out of nowhere.

Jangka is its own mini-world perched at 11,550 feet. At once a bustling hub for remote villages and in part a remote village itself, its 3,000 inhabitants range from Muslim Chinese business entrepreneurs to Tibetan farmers and nomads.

It does give you the feeling that it is unloved when you roll in. Dirty and uncared for. Those who don't call it home generally leave just as fast as they come, and there's nothing much to attract anyone here. Garbage litters the street, and grime covers the broken windows of the few tiny restaurants scattered down the main street - the only street - of town.

Bloody animal hides fill up the sidewalks, drying in the sun, and mangy animals sniff around. It feels both crowded and too wide-open. Raw meat drapes over clotheslines and pig heads adorn stools to get the hair singed off by blowtorches. Visible filth is everywhere and on everyone.

But I love it. I love the life that has sprouted and grown in this utterly faraway and almost inaccessible location. In a place that seems unfit to live, there is life everywhere. Smiles fill up the entire faces of those roaming the streets, while their infectious laughter bubbles into the air. Nomads lick ice cream in the cold air with child-like fascination. Kids play with sticks and rocks and each other, their dirty faces looking more like too much fun than neglect. People stroll arm in arm, unafraid to let their affections be announced to anyone who passes them by. Everyone makes eye contact, reminding you that you are present, that you do matter, and that you are seen. The humanity taking up this place makes you glad to be alive and glad to be here in this moment in this place.

Shops selling the same thing have sprung up with hopes of wealth, and nomads eagerly call out and barter for items such as laundry soap, fabric, and big pots to place over their fires at home.

The wide river snakes through the middle of town, at times

quietly trickling its way down its route, but sometimes with such force, the water explodes over the rocks with a deafening roar. Kids splash naked in its pools when the sun warms the air enough to tolerate its bite.

In summer, the vegetable market is a splash of color calling to people who have weathered months and months of winter with nothing fresh entering their mouths. It feels like tangible hope and is bustling with promise.

This place is a crossroads. A crossroads of people and livelihoods and trade and spindly roads that lead deeper and deeper into the remote regions of the Himalayas. A crossroads of lives and experiences and hope for new opportunities.

It's a crossroads for me, too. It's a place where I will have to look myself in the face and decide who I am, what I believe, and how I should live. I'll have to face my fears and figure out why they are fears and how I will deal with them. I'll have to see my weakness, own my mistakes, and move forward.

A typical main street in a small, Tibetan town

CHAPTER 15

*B*omo is a colorful, outrageous, and lovely woman who has no name. In Tibetan culture, the high monks give babies names, not their parents. She was missed and was never given a proper name for some reason. She is literally known as "Older Sister Girl." She was always up to unpredictable antics, bordering on scandalous at times. Whether catching her unloading all of her trash that she had wheeled blocks down the road to dump into the town's river or flirting with an older Chinese man, she always kept us shocked and often laughing right along with her.

She had turned her home into a guesthouse of sorts, much like everyone else, but Bomo's had become my favorite guesthouse because she kept electric blankets on the beds. I was grateful for this even when I visited in the summer months. While the summer days could be warm, only needing a T-shirt but also sunscreen to protect from the intense, high-altitude rays, the evenings could be too cool, and the nights undisguisedly cold. She also had flushable squatty potties, a pretty awesome perk.

Of course, electricity and water were sporadic, rendering these perks useless much of the time, but when they existed, they could make all that was wrong feel right again.

The small courtyard gave the place its charm to me, as it seemed like sunlight liked to pool itself there during the daytime hours. Even in the winter months, I could drag a wooden table and chair into the middle of the courtyard to catch the warmth while a revolving door of locals came to try and teach me how to speak as they did. Even when snow covered the ground, just having our winter parkas, some hot tea, and the glorious high-altitude sun would thaw me enough to feel happy. Outdoors was warmer than indoors, anyway.

In December, Jangka had a high temperature of forty-seven degrees Fahrenheit and a low temperature of *negative* fifteen degrees Fahrenheit. Yes, it could get very, very cold.

Bomo loved to sit in on my makeshift classes. She would make up story after story about her visits to the many different countries of the world. She had never left her town, but her stories of venturing to the far-to-reach places were always dramatic and exciting. She wove a detailed account of all of her experiences that were so original that it did seem possible she had come from another planet altogether, one that was full of intrigue and adventure.

She also loved to burp. You know, belch. Before she speaks, after she speaks, and yes, even while she speaks, barreling through her words at the same time as she lets out the thunderous sound. She is the reason I learned to say, "That woman is a real burper" in Tibetan without intentionally trying to learn it, as my teacher repeated it so many times during our lessons.

There was no need for an alarm clock at Bomo's place, as the army base was located just next door, with warm-up exercises each morning, complete with the shouting of slogans as they worked their physical bodies. Monks were often heard chanting in those early hours, although I could never quite figure out where they were located.

Bomo was so happy to see that I had wed since my last visit and was thrilled to let us settle into her guesthouse for the long haul. She couldn't figure out why we didn't have a baby yet, and she tried to raise my spirits (which were just fine where they were) by telling me that slowly, slowly, it would come.

The first night at altitude continued to be hard for me. I didn't sleep, and the pain in my head was borderline unbearable. I had learned the hard way that it was essential to travel to altitude slowly, sleeping at height increments that allowed your body to adjust to the lack of oxygen present in the blood as you climbed higher and higher. I had accidentally pulled off a few incredibly dangerous stunts before I fully understood the necessary science to keep me healthy and alive. Now, although we traveled up the mountains at a safe speed, I still had to tough out the consequences for the first twelve to twenty-four hours.

The blanket on our bed wasn't big enough for two bodies. We laid our coats on top of us, but there was no way to stay warm enough for sleep to come. I comforted myself by believing that this would be the worst night. Things could only get better.

There could be accommodations; we'd just need to work through what they'd be.

A few days later, we watched the town spring to life with so many extra people that we went to inquire what was happening. The boarding school had been closed for the New Year holiday, and students were returning to school with their families from villages all over the county. People were crowding around shop windows to buy plastic basins to wash hands and faces and laundry soap for hand washing clothes in the school courtyard on days when the water was indeed flowing. We tried to find an empty table in a noodle shop, but this pint-sized town was having difficulty containing all of these bodies.

It was a unique experience watching this town known as a crossroads become a living, breathing version of that crossroads before our very eyes. So many men and women living out their histories and generations converging into one place all at once, gathering to work for a better future for their children and all who would follow after. The hope was palpable on those streets, in restaurants, and in front of those shop windows.

We, too, had so much hope for this place and these people. We settled in and developed rhythms and routines and pictured a new life in this place with grace and love and hope not only for others but also for ourselves and what part we would now play in the story that was being written. The hope in our hearts was palpable, too.

And then one day, with a lot of commotion and stress and very abruptly, we were asked to leave immediately by those who gave or withheld permission in this town. We were stunned when the door to our private room in the guesthouse flew open, and three police officers searched our room and questioned us.

All of our interactions with them up to this point caused us to believe that our plan to live in this place would happen. That we could confidently nestle into the happenings of this town, and with the amount of time that had elapsed, we had let dreams settle profoundly into our beings, so much so that the possibility of them being taken back felt preposterous and not possible.

The officials were kind and generous, to their credit, and assured us it would just be for a while, but we knew that this directive was more significant than we wanted to believe, cocooned in words a bit soft on the ears but with no less force.

It's hard not to be wanted in a place where you want nothing more than to be wanted. While there were so many factors at play and forces at work, it felt very personal even though, in all likelihood, it probably wasn't personal at all. They were people doing their jobs, jobs that allowed them to support their families and contribute to society. Hopefully, they also enjoyed those jobs, even when some aspects of them were a bit difficult.

But this was one of the first big moments when I felt like my dreams were being chipped away. How do we hold on to dreams and work for them and fight for them, all the while knowing that it's not just up to us?

It felt like this opportunity was a once-in-a-lifetime opportunity, given directly to me, received wholeheartedly, and just when I grabbed hold of it, it slipped right through my fingers, and I was left shocked. It felt more like someone had ripped it from my hands, and I had a hard time not trying to point fingers and blame whatever I could. It felt unfair. Cruel, even.

When I had entered China, I had knowingly signed away many of the freedoms we have come to expect as Americans. In China, things are done differently, and I thought I had been prepared for that. They had graciously allowed me to be a guest in their country, and following their rules was a part of the deal, and I did desire to be respectful and deferential, but I still found my insides bucking at this wildly divergent system more often than I would have liked.

It was hard not to hold a grudge, no matter how unwarranted and inexcusable that was on my part. I felt cheated. The power they had to control my life felt unfair to someone who had plans to control her own destiny and take life by the horns. All of the rules and regulations about how and when I could do things made me feel degraded and infuriated. It goes without saying that this was a bad attitude to harbor under my smiling exterior.

We drove down the road, away from this new sparkling chapter of life, shut down before we hardly began.

And I was mad.

CHAPTER 16

I carried that anger back with me smack dab on my lap on that bus over the two days it took us to arrive back into the city that was willing to keep us, although I wondered if they, too, all just wished we'd go home. I moped around like an unwanted guest that didn't want to be a guest anyway. We stopped at roadside stands along the way, and we ate dried ramen noodles right out of the bag and bit off bites of cucumber to round out the meal. If we were lucky, sometimes someone would reach their arm through the window with boiled eggs for sale. We'd stop once, and lunch would be ladled out of a big pot resting on one burner that we weren't sure what it was but was worth the few cents it cost to give it a go.

We often would pass accidents along the way, and this frequency was quite disturbing. It was intensified by the fact that it would take emergency personnel quite a long time to arrive if they even arrived at all.

Car sickness seemed to be a thing for most, even if it hadn't happened before. The winding mountain roads at fairly high speeds were enough to do a number on anyone.

It was a relief to make it to our destination, but after the lens I used to view the gentleness and lightheartedness of the Tibetan world, arriving back in the city felt too hard and too loud, and too abrasive. The city somehow felt even dirtier and colder than Jangka, and the smog that hung in the air felt suffocating.

There's nowhere to hide away in that city. While the mountains offer endless expanses of rolling hills with not a person in sight, the people are everywhere in the city, and the green spaces are nowhere. Any speck of green will most definitely have a sign saying you are not allowed to set foot on the grass and a uniformed security guard making sure that you don't.

I thought a place of our own would soothe my grumblings, especially after months of constant travel. We searched for apartments to rent, each one splattered with rat poop. I told the chain-smoking real estate agent that my main priority was to find a home without rats, which was becoming a hill I was willing to die on.

Instead of slowly getting used to facing them once in a while, their presence or absence had become almost an obsession for me. The agent's eyes flickered with annoyance, and he told me that was not possible, rats just *were*, and my anger toward this place and people rose right alongside my anxiety.

We took an almost cozy, almost tiny eighty square meter apartment with lots of wood trim to offset the cold, hard cement for USD 165 in rent a month. Everything seemed miniature, as I could stand in one place in the kitchen and touch all four walls.

That also included the washing machine wedged right across from the camping-sized stove, taking up half of the counter space.

We laughed after we had been carrying on a conversation about which bath mat to buy in the store because we weren't sure the small spot between the toilet and the shower and the sink could squeeze in the smallest mat the place had to offer. The fluorescent blue couch filled up the living room space, and the two bedrooms came with small desks wedged into the corners where we could get our work done under the windows, which were covered in bars to ward off potential intruders. But, to match the story I was feeding my brain, it was another symbolic sign that I was held against my will in a place I was desperate to leave behind for the real land I had come to walk upon. My beloved Jangka.

The home was supposed to be perfectly ours. A place to unload our suitcases after too much travel and a place to close the door when we needed a minute alone. But I seemed never to be able to find that quiet aloneness I was craving. The neighbors' every move could be heard through the wall, as well as the thousands of people just outside our window, going about their daily business.

I grew to resent my surroundings. A car alarm would make me seethe. The knife sharpener calling out his services over and over grated on my ears. Young lovers spatting rattled my brain. I took issue with strangers on the street who raced me for a taxi or employees who seemed like they chose not to assist me out of spite, although it's possible they were only nervous or didn't even know I was expecting them to help.

I wanted to love God and love people. That was my constant refrain. After meeting and knowing the inhabitants of Jangka, I couldn't help but think that *they* were the ones I was meant to love. Loving them had been easy, and I naturally and earnestly enjoyed my interactions with them. Happy and kind and hospitable and friendly and FUN. I *wanted* to be friends with them. I genuinely, sincerely enjoyed them.

Teacher Sunshine, Bomo, Sona, Father Ogden. They felt like the people God had sent me to love. And I was hoping to do that from right next door. I wanted to bump elbows with them as we washed our clothes in the river. I wanted to cook momos over my *own* fire while my guests sipped butter tea at *my* house. I wanted to chit-chat in the streets over the latest town news, and I wanted to share sorrows and joys and comfort them with the hope of Jesus. I wanted to be folded into the fabric of their lives.

I wanted to be so much a part of that town that those living there would embrace me as one of their own, losing my foreignness and instead becoming one of them. I wanted to share their spaces and have them share my spaces and have it feel like the most natural thing in the world.

But how can I bump elbows with them from ten hard travel hours away?

Being forced to postpone a dream, feeling its loss more powerfully because of its backdrop against a place I didn't want to be, forced me to confront things in my heart that were easier to set aside when things were going my way. Bummer that it usually works like that.

The stark difference in both of these places, these people, and the attitude in my heart was so obvious that I had no choice but to look at it. To examine it. To deal with it.

I'm ashamed to say that I think I truly saw the Chinese people themselves as an obstacle. Instead of being people to love, they became something to be endured while I got to the real work that mattered. The people felt like inconveniences, getting in my way and making my life harder.

The fact of the matter was that we had been met with a roadblock to the plans and desires that we had for ourselves. We did acknowledge that since this had occurred, our good and loving Heavenly Father had a different plan in mind, one we just couldn't see or understand yet. It was just trying to be grateful for this different plan that had my undies in a total bundle.

In hindsight, roadblocks often show themselves to be stepping stones rather than obstructions. A forced time to stop. To pause and consider where you've been, what you've done, mistakes, and changes that need changing.

And here's the thing I was faced with: If I couldn't love those right in front of me, what right did I have to think I could love those far away? Something needed to change. For my sake, for my Chinese neighbors, but most of all, for God's sake.

After a particularly bad day of culture shock during my first year, I ran the stairs of my seventeen-story apartment building and listened to a sermon on my MP3 player. The speaker prayed, "Don't let me live an hour past when I can give you glory." I remember thinking…I might be in trouble. How many of my actions that day had been glorifying to God? How many of my actions had not? And why was this even an issue? I was embarrassed at my self-centeredness.

As I read stories of other cross-cultural workers, I felt so ashamed of myself—so many examples of loving people so purely even when they were so strongly despised and persecuted. Here I was, having such a hard time trying to be civil to people that just wanted to chat with me and be my friend. I resented them feeling the freedom to ask me any personal question they wanted while berating me for simple things like marrying so late in life (twenty-eight!) or laughing out loud at my inability to strike a good enough deal with vendors or chiding me about mistakes I made trying to speak their native tongue.

I wondered if there would ever be enough grace in my heart to love this country. The pain it had been through had left ugly scars across all of its surfaces, and sometimes I just wanted to look away instead of love.

I read through the gospels in a desperate attempt for help, watched Jesus navigate a world that was not His own, and paid attention to how He handled it. I could see my life on the pages. He wanted to be alone, and the people found Him anyway. His response? This is the reason why I came. Such compassion and selflessness. He always saw the people, not how they had inconvenienced Him. He was humble. He resisted temptation. He did not receive thanks for His service and often did whatever came across His path. He was patient—so many things on this list that I could not say about myself.

The thing that finally lodged itself into my heart that helped me pull out of this terrifying funk was remembering that every person I felt had wronged me or had gotten in my way had their very own story. They cried, and they laughed, and they mourned, and they rejoiced. They were people, too. Individuals.

And we've all got parts of us that are hard to love. Myself very much included. Probably too much included. Some of us are better at keeping it tucked away and out of sight than others.

I had an opportunity. To be right here, right now, wherever right here happened to be. I was not in Jangka. But I was right here. This opportunity in this space in time would never come again. It could not be squandered. How many things would I miss along the way if I looked for something else?

God spoke to my heart, and I knew that as well as loving God with my whole heart, I must also learn to love my neighbor as myself. And it was becoming evident to me that it was something I would need to take time to learn and put into practice because it was somehow not coming naturally to me, unfortunately.

I must learn, for it had not or would not just happen. I must learn to feel the pains they had felt and continue to feel. The hardships they have endured, what they have survived, and what they have come through. I must learn compassion. I must learn humility. My way of doing life isn't the best because it's my way and all I've known.

I must learn to live here and live here well.

My baby step attempt was to focus on one individual at a time, trying to see whatever might lay just beyond the surface of what I seemed to think they were projecting outwardly. And it was true that the more I got to know a person, the brighter spot they became in my Chinese living. They were delightful, come to find out.

Any time I stopped at the convenience store just below my apartment, I would leave with a smile from my interaction with the always jolly Mr. Shopkeeper and his wife. When my Chinese tutor spent the weekend at my house, it was not because she was looking for cash or because I was looking for a free practice session. It was because we genuinely enjoyed each other's company. When the neighbor with the baby who was always outside our complex entrance playing when I left or returned stopped to greet me, and we chatted for a bit, the smiles exchanged between the three of us lingered on my face as I went about my business. Even taxi drivers lost their harsh edge when I asked them about their families and pictured them returning to their spot after a long day's work.

And I dared to start living just a little more like them, no matter how weird it felt at first. Not only was I now slurping tea like everyone else and throwing dirty napkins and chicken bones on the floor of the restaurant, but I started using my elbows to move my way forward at the grocery store. It was uncomfortable for me, but soon enough, it helped me feel like I was part of the group, and once you're a bit more on the inside, everything that seemed so wildly abrasive before starts to feel much less so. Once I lightened up, I could see that they already were lightened up, and I had read way too much into the situation in the first place.

Seeing the prejudice in my heart was necessary for my journey, no matter how much shame I had to endure. It was the first step toward change as I navigated a culture so different from the only one I had known. It didn't mean that I was transformed overnight. It was still a daily struggle. But one that I acknowledged. I declared its existence, and I weakened its power.

When I felt cheated or disrespected, I looked into that person's eyes and saw them as a fellow human being. I remembered that they had favorite foods and were wearing a flowered scarf, possibly given to them by someone who loved them. I remembered that somewhere along the line of their life, they had experienced deep sorrow. And it had left its mark. And I could choose to lift that burden just a little or add to it.

Would I speak life or death to this person standing before me?

They say the journey is more important than the destination. In my fight to love the people of Jangka in the way I wanted to love them, I was learning that love had a lot more to offer than simple smiles and a shared meal. It was seeing the rough parts of a person and not leaving. In acknowledging their place of belonging in this minute on this corner of the sidewalk in this particular interaction that would never happen again. It was in declaring by my actions that they mattered.

I was learning to be present. Wherever present happened to be. In whatever situation, present happened to be. That each moment itself contained an important choice.

I was learning what it meant to love.

CHAPTER 17

*I*n the end, what we feared was a major setback turned out to be not that big of a deal after all, and after much too much whining and complaining and striving and fretting on my part, just two months later, on a gloriously sunny day, we found ourselves welcomed back by the officials with what strangely seemed to be open arms.

The unpredictability of this kind of thing, in some ways, gave us great joy when we were least expecting it. Still, it also forced us to live with a bit of apprehension about any and every situation, no matter how seemingly small. It never felt like tomorrow was a given. It was a somewhat disconcerting way to live, waiting for the other shoe to drop.

Or, I guess you could say it was a wonderful way to live. A forced living in the present and being grateful for whatever opportunities were given. It was a chance to keep our eyes open and search for all of the good that was to be had whenever it happened to arrive, which was very frequent if we took the time to acknowledge it.

We found a room to rent in a big Tibetan stone house. The room we rented was large and even had shelving built into the wall for our few belongings. An entire wall of Tibetan-style windows let in lots of natural light, and I felt happy. The room was clean, bright, and colorful, and we even had access to a shared sink, squat toilet, and shower at the end of the hall.

It was on the edge of town, and this very typical home sat on the only through street, rising majestically in its perfection. Row after row of flat rock had been laid on top of each other, layer after layer, to complete a fortress of beauty. Intricate and bright paintings framed the windows, and it looked itself to be a piece of art.

A Chinese businessman and his wife had rented out the bottom floor to serve as a restaurant, selling rice and stir-fried vegetables and pork when it was available. The Tibetan owners of the home had their living quarters on the same floor as what would be our new home. Their main home was in a village about 30 minutes away, but they were trying to run a guest house for Chinese tourists, albeit seemingly unsuccessfully.

The truth is that there was just very little to see in this town. A quick overnight stop for a Chinese tour bus happened on rare occasions as they tried to make their way to some of the bigger and more attractive Tibetan towns. Still, all of the buses rolled into another guesthouse in town, unfortunately located just across the road from what we began to affectionately call our rental, ShiDa's Guesthouse. Maybe this was extra painful, as ShiDa had to continually watch her dreams unfold right in front of her eyes but granted to someone else. So close, yet so very far away.

ShiDa is probably the most lovable person you will meet in this book.

There is nothing not to like. She is simple and sweet and funny and kind. Her giant of a husband adores her; his stoic presence ruffled once in a while from a belly laugh that escapes involuntarily due to some or another shenanigan of his unpredictable and excellently unequaled wife. Her Tibetan robes hung perfectly from her tiny body, and her hair was braided with ribbon and wound tightly around her head. Her gold earrings hung heavily from her lobes and gave her the look of a lost princess from a forgotten place long ago.

Her simple joy in life was contagious. She loved hearing stories from across the ocean. Once she learned that a wife would often take her husband's last name instead of her own in America, a custom we do not share with Tibet, she started calling me by Ethan's Tibetan name to great amusement to herself. I'd open my eyes early in the morning, and there she'd be, standing over my bed, her face inches from mine, with a gleeful smile on her face calling me her new pet name for me.

She loved to try and trick me, often using the same tactics, never caring that I had caught on to her ploys a ways back. After running out alone, she'd greet me and tell me Ethan wasn't home yet when I'd return home. When I rounded the corner into our room to see him sitting there, she would howl with laughter. This favorite game of hers never lost a morsel of joy for her.

She was hilarious, sometimes on purpose, sometimes not.

She always got her animals mixed up, which never seemed to get less funny. She'd call a goat a sheep or a pig a cow.

She would fill our plates with potato momos. Mashed potatoes rolled into a thin layer of bread and dipped in spices. I could eat them all day. Cooking was an incredible talent she possessed. She had a genuine good-naturedness, which made her completely easy to be around.

Her 20-year-old son was himself a character, which I guess should come as no surprise. He had been sent to a monastery at a young age by the family, as is often the case. One son is chosen as an offering for the family; another may be sent to school, another learns to farm or drive a car or provide another source of income for the family.

However, this particular son's thirst for adventure and trouble made him decide the monastic life was not for him, and he had returned home in his late teens just to be a boy or a man. I often wondered how that would have felt for the family, but outwardly, there was no indication of frustration, sadness, or disappointment. It seemed he was a joy to his family, just as he was. His first question to us was, "Is it true that there are rivers of Pepsi and Sprite in America, and you can drink them for free whenever you like?" When we said, nope, sorry, he got animatedly angry and yelled, "Man! Those LIARS!"

We absolutely adored this family, which was a very good thing, as they came in and out of our room whenever they liked, no knocking whatsoever! They loved to watch us. What I mean is, like you would watch a television show. They would burst into our room, pull up a plastic stool, and just watch.

One time they watched for four hours straight, not even a bathroom break. It was a Sunday, a day we took to rest, recover from the past week, and prepare and plan for the upcoming week. We played some cribbage and invited them to join in. ShiDa wasn't interested in playing, but she oohed and aahed over the two gold and two silver pegs on the cribbage board at various intervals throughout the afternoon.

She would continually exclaim loudly and interject that she didn't know how to do anything. Nothing at all. Loud laments and wailings that she didn't know how to watch TV. The TV programming was in the Chinese language, which she didn't understand or speak, and she said the pictures themselves moved too fast to follow. "I can't read letters," she'd cry! "I don't know numbers," she'd yell! "So, I just clean," she declares!

And clean she does, which makes this place feel very different from many we have stayed in before. She sweeps and sweeps and sweeps some more.

While we played our game, she spent quite a lot of time pretending to read *David Copperfield* by Charles Dickens. We tended to bring thick books to the mountains, as we were limited in our luggage and tried to get the most bang for our buck. She held the book upside down as she read. When she was done, she began her laments again about how she couldn't read Chinese. I decided not to tell her that particular book was written in English.

One day, ShiDa's son returned home announcing that he had gotten caught by the police for having no papers for his car and no license. ShiDa was so mad, but not about him not having a license and yet driving. Of course, he didn't have one, and she didn't care, but she was mad because, in her opinion, he had driven too far away. She said, "We know all the police here; stay close; they won't get you in trouble. Those police far away; we don't know them, so we don't know what they'll do." He was charged 400 Kuai, the equivalent of about 50 USD.

Imagine my surprise very early the next morning when ShiDa was banging on our door, telling us to get up because we were going to "play" in the car! Her son was a maniac driver, which we got to experience firsthand. Also, knowing he didn't have a license was a concern to me, even though that was commonplace out here. At one point, he swerved to stop quickly to show us the spot on the road where someone had recently pulled a guy out of his car, killed him, and then had driven off! I was relieved to spill myself out into the summer festival in ShiDa's hometown, for which we all were awakened.

I wonder why advance notice is not something given in most contexts out there. Is it superstition? Is it that they don't have a plan until just that moment? In any case, the day before, I had no idea this elaborate event was happening, but there I was today.

Carpe Diem.

This festival was a repeat of what we were coming to experience regularly. I loved checking out the clothing choices of all of the celebrators. Festival time brought out everyone's finest, and Tibetans left no body part unchecked. From their shoes to their hair accessories, they were complete masterpieces. I wore my only skirt with a sweater and put on earrings for the occasion.

ShiDa was, of course, the life of the party, cracking jokes and making everyone laugh. It seemed everyone else enjoyed her just as much as we did. She paraded us around and mothered us, ensuring we were warm, content, and almost uncomfortably fed. We learned a phrase from her that day that we still say regularly, over a decade later.... "I'm on my way!" Okay, so the phrase itself may not be new, but how dear ShiDa used it was! People would call her to their tent, ask her to join them and bring her bubbly life into theirs, and she would call out, "I'm on my way!" just as she passed them by. We soon found out that she never had any intention to stop or return or visit at all. It was her way of acknowledging them while also doing what she wanted to do.

People weren't shy around us, and we found ourselves in the middle of many interesting and insightful conversations. They wanted to understand us just as we wanted to understand them. Topics ranged from food to family and into hard things, too.

As cheerful and merry as ShiDa was, she couldn't escape the brutal harshness of this life any more than anyone else. We found out that day that three of her siblings had already died, all from alcohol abuse. It was interesting to note that although we had watched her cry real tears out of fear from an eclipse that we had all encountered together, she told us very matter-of-factly and with no apparent sadness at all that one of her siblings had fallen drunk into a stream face first and drowned. Everyone continued snacking and smiling, and we were so shocked by what appeared to be such a casual attitude toward death. As we finished up the celebratory day, it seemed that this attitude toward death was born out of necessity and reality.

Freak accidents seemed not so freak out here, and we often

heard stories of people falling to their death from a horse or a roof or even merely dying in the middle of the day from something they just called stomach sickness.

Death seemed to be much quicker, simpler, and almost contagious out here, and it seemed to lurk around every corner. One night, I stumbled out of our room into the dark hallway and began to make my way to the bathroom. The door next to ours was open, and ShiDa and her husband were huddled around their window. They called me in and told me to look outside. Although it was dark, I could see the outline of a body sprawled in the middle of the road. They told me it was a monk, but I already knew. The robes were visible from the window.

A dump truck was parked on the road, and the monk had run straight into it on his motorcycle. I could see his sneakers peeking out from under his crimson robes, giving him a personality and realness. Shoes that walked the town streets earlier today would now have no more use.

My insides were twisted up with this horror unfolding before my eyes, but ShiDa was so calm and confident that this was karma doing its job. If a monk dies a bad death, he had lots of sin, she explained. She said you could tell a bad monk or a good monk just by looking, and it seemed there were plenty of both. She said if the monk is playing in town, riding motorcycles, and playing cards, they're not good. If they stay in the monastery and help people, they're good.

What was this monk doing, ShiDa said, on a motorcycle so late at night? She said this must be part of his karma, and she was satisfied with the circle of life working itself out.

Good and bad deeds are a central part of a Tibetan's existence. It seemed to always be on the mind, this constant working to rid yourself of sin and gird yourself with righteousness. You can see the practical effort to accumulate merit, or good deeds, almost anywhere you look. Prayer beads being worked in the hands of most elderly people, prayer wheels lining the many monasteries, stacks of stones placed on hillsides, or prayers carved into stones or wood almost everywhere. There is a relentless pursuit of merit happening at any given time in the Tibetan nooks and crannies of our globe.

The honor given to any living thing is a bit surprising when faced with what seems to be a casual attitude toward death. Still, great care is given to avoid directly killing animals or even insects. When ShiDa would rant and wail at those tour buses that stopped across the road instead of frequenting her place of business, to place her disappointment on something specific, she would yell, "They eat fish!" It was the worst accusation she could come up with. Taking the life of a small animal to feed yourself was horrific to the Tibetans. A yak was a much more appropriate food source, as the physical size of the animals helped feed many, many people.

Karma taking its designated course or not; there was now a dead body in the road in front of our house. This is not first and foremost about me; however, having a dead body right outside your window is more than unsettling. Especially because Tibetans believe that after a person dies, you cannot move the body for three days to allow the spirit to exit the body completely. During this time, monks chant over the body and take time to tell the person that they have died and cannot go to their home or other places they used to frequent. The monks also go to the deceased's home and the homes of his friends and relatives to write a symbol on their door that reminds the spirit of the dead to go away.

So, for three days, a deceased man was lying on the road in front of our house. All kinds of rituals were performed; sprinkling stuff, burning stuff, laying paintings on the road, bending over the body, ringing bells, and hanging scarves in the trees. They put a nomad tent around the man, which completely blocked over half of the road - the *only* road going anywhere else in all of the prefecture! Such was the importance of this ritual.

Meanwhile, the family daily burned food outside of their home for the spirit of the dead. The smell is believed to fill up their bellies and ward off hunger. After forty-nine days, the person is reborn.

This town is tiny, but there are constantly big things going on, leading to what appeared to me to be an excessive amount of death. From amongst their 3000-person population, at least five people die in fights and ten in car accidents every year. Natural disasters claim many lives at once. A landslide killed sixty in the county next to us while we sat drinking our instant coffee packets mixed with hot water.

Even though it seems rare out here, cancer is known as the disease that kills people who live by the ocean. It works quickly when it does strike, as diagnostic tools are not available. A guest house owner in the next town over where we often stayed received news of her cancer, just six days before she died at the age of fifty before we could pass through and see her gentle and smiling face for one last time.

Sometimes we live out our days oblivious to the inevitability of death. We are confident that the claws of destruction are not strong enough or close enough to reach us or those we love as we laugh and play and dart about the enormous surface area of our full and happy lives.

And then sometimes we live out our days feeling suffocated by death.

Out here, death feels relentless and alive, its breathing presence hovering just above your shoulder.

Sometimes it's hard to know the best way to keep living while the dying die around us.

Because out here, it felt like everyone just kept dying.

A Tibetan house made out of stone

CHAPTER 18

*T*he fragility of life was an ever-present thought, and matters of death seemed to come up regularly in conversation, and now we could understand why. This life out here was just so full of it. One day, the four-year-old nephew of a friend of ours fell off a roof and died. We heard of a fight in the town next door where three people were killed over the equivalent of three US dollars.

Two sisters ran a restaurant in town, offering homemade chewy noodle soup for less than a dollar, which promised to fill your belly, warm your body, and guarantee you'd be back for more later. One of the sisters had a toothache, steadily growing worse. This was, of course, greatly unfortunate since out here there was nothing to be done except to alleviate the pain with powders that came folded into small squares of paper, handed out by the local medicine man.

While she tried to forget her discomfort, she asked me if I "mani don" when a person dies.

These are the prayers offered for the safe passage of the

deceased person's soul onto their next life in the process of rebirth. After death, a person's good deeds would be weighed against their bad deeds, and this process decides whether their next rebirth would be into a more favorable situation (for example, a woman could become a man in their next life) or into a more negative position (such as becoming an insect). Of course, this is a matter of utmost importance.

And here's where the rubber meets the road because death is the final line that can't be crossed again in Christianity. No second life, no second chances.

I want to tell her about the hope of eternal life with Jesus. I want to tell her about heaven. About a place filled with everything good and right and just as all was meant to be. A place where joy fills all corners and sadness has long been forgotten. Where love is all there is and pain does not exist, and there is room enough for her. And for me. And the endless cycle of rebirth does not exist or have power, and there is rest.

And I do tell her.

But sometimes, I feel like my confidence waivers. My pride has been sanded down to understand that I might not have everything just right. And speaking about the afterlife feels like the most extreme example of this since I've never been there. The ground I had stood on so confidently before felt like it made my legs wobble a wee bit.

It would take time, experiences, and real life before I was ready and confident enough to let my genuine, authentic, messy faith be fully on display. It would be a while before I even knew and saw and understood that my faith was messy and not quite as tidy as I had thought it was or had wanted it to be in the first place.

This was before I learned that I could believe and share the things I held on to while also acknowledging that I might not be entirely right about everything, and there was room for questions.

I recently heard a friend tell someone who was scared to die that she didn't need to be scared. She could trust in Jesus as her savior, and she wouldn't need to be afraid of what came next anymore. I sat up a little straighter in my chair while I felt a little funny in the tummy. As a Christian, maybe I'm not supposed to fear death. But I do.

Death and the afterlife feel way too unknown for my comfort level. Too unknown for me to set fear aside. I don't like surprises. I'm one of those people who went into my bedroom and shut the door and cried when my mom pulled off an epic surprise sweet sixteenth birthday bash. I want to know all there is to know about all there is to know. And that includes what happens on the other side of death. I don't know what it will be like when the breath leaves my body, and I go on to whatever there is to go on to. And it freaks me out. A bit. Sometimes a lot. I want to know.

And, of course, there's the threat of hell. The very thing that caused me to crawl into my mama's bed late at night and ask Jesus to come into my heart because I was NOT going to go to THAT place. Add into the mix confusing songs like "No You Can't get to Heaven on Roller Skates" and "Heaven is in my Heart." I'm not exactly sure I knew what I was doing. Still, when my mom asked me if I was ready to ask Jesus into my heart, I stopped worrying about how He was going to get in there and if He was that small and grabbed on to that piece of hope that would keep me away from the flames licking at my heels.

I remember hearing about the streets of gold. The mansions that awaited us and the crowns filled with jewels that would be ours, but those weren't things that felt motivating to me, and I also was confused about why those things were considered worldly down here, but then we were supposed to want it once we got through earth's phase of the journey. I remember lying in bed as a kid and trying to think about forever. Oh, it almost made me nauseous.

So how do I explain the afterlife when I don't even have adequate words in English to help my head wrap itself around it?

What comes next after this life is a significant question. For everyone.

Some people go through life with the view that this life is just a test, and the real stuff comes after. Some people go through life with the belief that this is the only thing there is.

At that moment, faced with talking about things that I couldn't be specifically sure of, I knew that the thing I did have was hope. Faith. The belief that what is wrong CAN be made right again.

And that was something I was ready to give. Not perfectly. Not without some doubts and questions rubbed into the mix, but that felt sincere. Genuine.

When I looked at this woman, holding her face and trying to eat a bowl of soup, I saw a person with deep questions, longings, and unmet hopes. I saw a person who experienced simple days, crabby days, and milestone moments. I saw a person who was growing and learning and searching and changing. I saw a person who just wanted to get through the day sometimes and someone who tried to put her nose to the grindstone on another. I saw someone just like me.

At that moment, we were just two people, not all that different after all. A barley farmer living under a mountainside making noodles while her yaks grazed and her children rolled tires down a dusty track of road. A young woman traveling the world with coffee packets hidden in her backpack and goodwill in her heart with a mother worrying about her safety from thousands of miles away. Two women eating soup for lunch on a Thursday in June.

I continued to grow in learning how to see people after my hard-fought mini victory in the big city. I was moving past successfully seeing people as individuals but also learning to look at them not as I assumed they were or should be or what they could be one day—but just looking at them as they were today. Right now. Tired. Sad. Happy. Simple. Complicated. Friendly. Searching. Doubting. Alive.

And reaching out a hello and saying, I see you. I'm here too, in this big world next to you. Should we stand together for a while? Declaring with my actions and sometimes my words that I would accept her just as she was in whatever moment she happened to be.

To let her know that even if this was all she was and all she'd ever be, it was more than enough.

I did long for people to come to know Jesus. I did. But I

now knew that even if they didn't, their value would remain the same in my eyes, heart, actions and care. It was not my power of persuasion that would draw them to Jesus. My words couldn't guarantee an outcome of any sort.

That was between her and the God-above-all-gods, His Son, and the Holy Spirit.

But I could let her be herself and allow her to let her guard down and lay all her cards on the table with confidence that I wouldn't turn away. And more than that, show her that I was willing to lay my cards on the table. Honestly. I was not trying to paint my life and beliefs as a perfectly crafted specimen that would be impossible to be refused. But just as they were. Messy, complicated, confused at times, but hopeful.

To show her that I could breathe through the hard moments because of the anchor of my soul. To show her that many answers felt like they were just beyond my reach, but there was enough to make me feel sure, certain. Enough to help me keep putting one foot in front of the other and offering my hand to those I met along the way, sharing the hope that was in me, the gospel of Jesus Christ.

I was thankful for the book of 1 Peter and his words that reminded me always to be ready to share this hope that was in me, but also reminded me to do it with gentleness and respect. Navigating that was not as straightforward as it appeared to be. It looked simple, sitting there smushed into one beautifully crafted verse in the Bible. I wasn't sure it was simple, but I was discovering that not only could it be done, but it was a beautiful way through - the only way through.

CHAPTER 19

*E*ach time we were presented with an opportunity to share Jesus, it was amazing how individualized the situation happened to be.

Like with Dashu, the monk.

One day, we received an invitation from a stranger, which had become a normal part of our everyday lives. We were often invited to have tea, a meal, or even stay overnight at someone's home after a brief greeting along the side of the road.

Which is precisely what happened on this particular day.

We joined a bunch of middle school students and their librarian and piled in a van headed for a small village an hour south of Jangka. We were handed a massive clump of roasted barley flour mixed with butter tea upon arrival, and the eating never stopped from there. We crowded close together inside brightly decorated tents while time and space were suspended in this alternate universe.

I chitter-chattered away as best as I could, and it seemed that we had become the central figures in this gathering in many ways. I continued to smile, nod, and give what felt like mini speeches to medium-sized groups of people. The hours rolled over on top of each other, and as I started to get tired, the connection between my ears and brain seemed like it kept glitching, and sometimes it felt like it stopped working altogether. While some people seemed easy to understand, others seemed to speak a completely unintelligible language. I would go from comfortably understanding certain sentences from the person sitting on my left without any effort to having sounds clash utterly foreignly from the person on my right.

How it took me most of one day to realize that the main dialect spoken in this village was something I had never even heard of before is astounding and kind of embarrassing, but there you have it. We had found ourselves right in the middle of a new language group, only 1 hour from our beloved Jangka.

This news rocked me over-dramatically, but I felt completely overwhelmed and discouraged. I had been pouring every little drop of my being into learning the language of Jangka, only to feel how limited it was in scope by going on a very short car ride where all of my efforts seemed to proclaim themselves null and void.

While some of the villagers could also speak the language of Jangka, primarily the teachers and government officials (which was part of the reason I was so slow to catch on to the accurate picture), the majority of the people could not.

So how then were they to be reached with the good news of Jesus? Ethan and I were two of only a very, very small handful of people studying the language of the Jangka Tibetans. Still, no one was learning the language of this beautiful and important and valuable and wonderful village. I wasn't sure if anyone even knew this place existed, let alone that they spoke a completely different dialect.

It's strange for me to think about people going about their lives today, somewhere on this planet, that are virtually unknown. Well, unbeknownst to humans. It gives me some solace to know that God knows them, and I am not privy to whatever tricks or plans He has up His sleeves. I find myself stuck on the fact that just as much as I was once a teenage girl attending high school in a suburb in the USA, these people were here, all along, living their lives just as much as I was living mine.

So here we were, in this unknown location where people spoke an unknown language that had never been written down, and while Ethan jumped into this challenge with a grin on his face and a smile in his heart, and new phrases escaping his lips, I pretty much threw in the towel. I was not up for the challenge of trying to sort through a third language in this country.

By hour thirty-one, we were exhausted. I noticed that it wasn't only me but that Ethan also hit his limit, which made him feel slightly more human in my eyes in that new linguistic information roller coaster. We begged to rest and started walking toward a newly-built home where we had been given the main room/kitchen as our sleeping quarters.

As we entered our guest's home, we realized that everybody else was entering our host's home as well, and they followed us right on up to our beds and plopped themselves beside us on the two wooden platforms. Ethan was so tired that he was sound asleep in a matter of seconds. On the other hand, I was a bit unsettled by being watched while I slept, so I decided I'd try a sudoku puzzle in a game book I had brought with me.

There is no way to miss Dashu when he walks into the room. His brightly colored yellow and burgundy robes swish back and forth as he slowly limps along. He is always smiling. His hunched back rises seemingly above the top of his head.

Funny enough, his nickname is "the American" because of his big nose and non-almond-shaped eyes. He crossed the room and came and sat next to me. Soon enough, I couldn't see my sudoku puzzle anymore because his head was in the way. He was a teacher at the elementary school in the village. More specifically, he wasn't *a* teacher; he was *the* teacher, as in the only one for all six grades.

I thought he might find the puzzle interesting, and since I couldn't see it anyway, I explained how to do it. The puzzle and pen were out of my hand before I knew what had happened. I looked for another pen to do a different puzzle. No other pen. The only other thing I had was my Bible, so I picked it up and began to read.

I was on Matthew chapter 13 and began with the parable of the sower. The words seemed to jump off the page as I thought about seeds falling all over this particular small village where I currently sat. It had never had a spiritual farmer pass through before, to my best guess. I thought about how the gospel goes forth and our little place in it.

Our little place felt not so little at that moment, as I worried about how long it would be before another farmer with seed would pass through.

Even Dashu could be the soil that might one day produce a hundredfold. Suddenly, at that moment, I was sure that Dashu *was* that soil, and I was desperate to get the seeds ready to plant. I was worried that my vocabulary was insufficient, and more than that, I questioned my place as a woman to share such vital things with a monk. So, I kept reading.

When I continued to read that the kingdom of heaven was like a mustard seed that a man took and sowed in his field, I started to get concerned. The Bible said that although it is the smallest of all seeds, it is larger than all the garden plants and becomes a tree when it has grown. Wouldn't it be great if Dashu was the mustard seed? Dashu *could* be the mustard seed. Dashu *is* the mustard seed. Full-blown panic set in. This chance to share with him could not be missed; I felt it so surely. The gospel could bring him life, and he could take that life to all of his students who spread out throughout these valleys, bringing transformation and peace to families, villages, and people groups.

It felt like this was a moment that had been prepared for us.

I woke up worn-out Ethan too soon for him to get any quality rest and said, "We have to tell Dashu about Jesus right now. But, can you do it, please?"

Just then, with his pen poised over his sudoku puzzle and with his eyes still on the page, Dashu began to talk about sin. He spoke of the different kinds of sin and those that leave you with no hope. These words were uttered just as I, myself, was contemplating the opposite: the bigness of the gospel and the hope available for all, and specifically for Dashu.

But there sat Dashu, declaring that he was a hunchback because of all of the evil deeds he had done in his past lives. The sin that left no way out for him to be anything other than a sinner, marked for life. The Buddhist doctrine of karma had convinced him that it was over for him before it even began. He was entering life with a deficit, obviously stated by his congenital disability, making his place on the ladder of rebirth clear to him and anyone who looked at him.

I immediately thought of the story in John chapter 9 about the man born blind. The disciples had asked Jesus who had sinned, the man or his parents, to cause this man to be born blind. Jesus said it wasn't that man's sin or the parents' sin that had caused this disability. It had absolutely nothing to do with what someone had done or not done. The purpose of his blindness was only that the works of God could be displayed in him. The purpose was grand, and it was no one's fault at all.

Here was hope, scratched into the words of God, held out for Dashu, a hunchback monk in a remote village in a communist country living among a people group no one knew about except themselves. These words were for him. Now.

And then, Ethan began, "A long, long time ago, there was nothing. No moon, no stars, no people, no nothing except for one thing. And the only thing that was was the God-above-all-gods. The God above all gods does not need anything; no clothes, no water. Instead, He Himself is the giver and sustainer of all life. He is good, and in Him, there is no evil.

God made man and woman and had a good relationship with them. The very best relationship. But one day, that man and woman disobeyed God, and because the God-above-all-gods is pure and has no sin, His relationship with man was broken. This is so sad because the God above all gods is love, and knowing Him and being with Him is right and good and wonderful.

But the God above all gods had a plan from the very beginning, and to save man and restore the relationship, the God above all gods sent His own Son, Jesus, into the world to be born as a baby. He was a human. But He was also God.

He was powerful and healed the sick, walked on water, cast out demons, and commanded the weather. He always did right and lived His entire life with no sin. Sin is doing what is wrong or not doing what is right according to God's rules.

Jesus chose to die for the sake of humankind and took our sin upon Himself, and then gave those who trusted in that sacrifice His very righteousness. Three days later, He rose from the dead, conquering both sin and death forever. If we put our faith in Jesus and His sacrifice, God sees us as having no sin. Our sin is erased and taken away, and we never have to think about it again because Jesus did away with it. The best thing is that we can be reconciled with the God above all gods, the God who is love, again."

Dashu listened intently to Ethan's story. Leaning in, eyes focused, hardly moving. However, as Ethan shared specifically about the man born blind, Dashu became physically agitated and began shaking his head. News about a creator of the world that he hadn't known about, information about a man who was God who lived a perfect life, and news about someone rising from the dead did not make him pause. Personally, it was the freedom offered to him that he couldn't get past or believe.

He loudly said, "No, my sin has made me this way." He said it with so much confidence that it almost sounded like pride, even though I can only imagine living with this belief would be akin to having the load of the world on your shoulders.

Ethan continued to gently share with him that there was a way to be free from the burden and slavery of sin, no matter how big that burden is or feels. That way is through Jesus Christ, but its impossibility was etched on this man's face, and the weight of this loss pulled and squeezed at the hearts in our chests.

We couldn't convince him. And yet that wasn't our job anyway. But it still stung. We could plant, hopefully water, but it was only God who could, in the end, make the plant grow and reproduce. While knowing and believing that does relieve some pressure, it is also hard to stomach at certain times. I want the power to make that seed grow. I want to have just the right words, and I want to say them just the right way with just the right tone at just the right time and then sit back and watch it grow.

But that didn't happen.

We never saw Dashu again, though it wasn't for lack of trying. We returned to that village, bringing parts of God's word, freshly printed to deliver to this unforgettable monk, but it was as if he had vanished into thin air.

That original burden that I felt to share the good news with him never left, and he was never far away from our prayers. I tell myself that those prayers may accomplish things that we will never know of, and I wonder if he's somewhere out there, living in freedom and scattering seeds among so many other unknown villages. Has his mustard seed of faith taken root? Has it grown to be so big that people can see it all over, coming closer to a better look? Finding hope and truth and settling into its branches?

In my heart, he will forever be known as Mr. Mustard Seed. I wonder if I will ever know what became of him, and if I don't, I guess all that's left is to trust God had a plan when we climbed into that van with a librarian and his students, and it's not for me to know what part of the story we were to play.

"The Kingdom of heaven is like a grain of mustard seed that a man took and sowed in his field. It is the smallest of all seeds, but when it has grown it is larger than all the garden plants and becomes a tree, so that the birds of the air come and make nests in its branches." Matthew 13:31-32

CHAPTER 20

The sorrows of this land did seep out everywhere once we had stuck around long enough to observe it. As intense as the joy was here that we regularly experienced, true to life, there was also plenty of sorrow to accompany it. As we followed a man to his home, it was hard not to stare at his shriveled arm. His clothes hung loosely from his frame, and his face looked older than it should have.

As soon as he had us settled on a bench-like seat, he launched into the justice system as his first matter of conversation. He wanted to know the consequences of killing a man in America. Would you go to jail?

He wanted to know because he had killed a man and had to spend 12 whole years in prison.

Yes, at that moment, I did feel uneasy, knowing that no one in the entire world had any idea where we were and that where we were was snuggly inserted into the quiet home of a self-professed murderer. I was trying to remember that everyone has a story, so don't be too quick to judge. I was also trying to keep my cool and be calm and keep my heart beating quietly enough that he wouldn't be able to hear it.

The man motioned to his shriveled arm and said the man he killed had first cut off part of his hand, and it was never fixed, so the arm itself had become completely unusable, hence what was visible before us now.

It seemed to me that not only had his arm become unusable but his very life. He told us that he had no hope as a murderer, and I recalled that Dashu the monk had also just explained to us this very thing, that murder is a sin that forever seals your fate. I didn't realize I would be given a chance to inspect this wide-ly-held belief so close and personally quite so quickly. It was true, this man told us. Tibetan Buddhism offers no freedom from a sin so dark as that.

What was it like, I wondered, to walk through life with the word murderer stamped on your forehead and your back and on your arm that was now shriveled and screamed *remember* to anyone who passed by? It called, *remember that I killed a man? Remember what I did?*

One moment in time, one tiny little moment, will now be the only moment. The moment that dictates the rest of this life and the one to come.

Did this man deserve to be forgiven?

I could picture him on that street corner. A very young man egged on by another, also too very young. A knife hung from his sash, just like all of the others surrounding him—a split-second choice. The blade perfectly placed or perfectly misplaced.

It was finished.

And now he sat before me, old, graying, and wrinkled. An arm so shriveled for so long that the before had almost ceased to exist. Almost. But I thought the before must also haunt him. Maybe even more than the moment when everything changed. Because the before was there, in all its glittering perfection, reminding him of how it could have been.

This man never left the streets of his youth. Here he was, standing before us decades later. Did he think about leaving? Did he even register that it was a choice? Or maybe it wasn't an option. Maybe there was no choice. Perhaps he didn't have money or connections or the strength and spirit it would take to go and build a new life for himself.

Maybe he knew that no matter where he went, he couldn't hide, that the truth was the truth, and that his arm would forever keep his deed on display.

Had he come to accept it? Did he offer the information that he killed a man at the beginning of every conversation so willingly as he had with us? Did he do it to get it out of the way or see who stuck around or because he couldn't be anything other than that one moment in his past?

Or maybe he had made peace. That this was just the way it was. It was said and done and couldn't hold power over him anymore, so he might as well declare it himself and own it valiantly and simply.

That man seemed so different from me, and not just his language or ethnicity, or lifestyle. He had lived dangerous moments. He had created dangerous moments on purpose. He had fought and killed and lived out twelve years in one of the most ruthless prisons in possibly the world. He seemed as different from me as could ever be possible.

But what word would be stamped on my life if my mistakes held physical evidence as much as this man's?

Maybe it wasn't as shocking. But still.

Was his flash of anger that marred his life and took another unforgivable while the things that clawed at my goodness remained excusable?

I wasn't sure it worked that way. But I also assumed and lived as if it did. Where was the line? Why did I feel like I was in one category, and he was in another? It seemed like this was how Buddhism looked at the situation, from what we had been told. It was easy for me to look at it that way too. I wanted to run and never look back and hide and stay far, far away, showing him that I didn't believe there was hope for him, either.

But was that true? Jesus' death was enough for this man, too, right? My mind said yes, while my heart shuddered and quaked. It's easy to believe something in theory, but when you're eyeing the large knives used for daily chores hanging on the wall opposite you while in this notable situation, it is quite another thing to live out those beliefs.

Life was getting messier and messier the more I let my eyes adjust to my surroundings. It seemed nothing was as explicit or conclusive as I thought it was at first glance—so many situations with so many questions and no easy answers.

But there, also in these surroundings, I saw something that made it all feel simple for a second. It was this man's silent wife, churning butter tea by hand in the corner. As she plunged the wooden dowel up and down and around the waist-high barrel, I saw a woman who chose to love a man who had killed.

When the world said there was no hope, she said, I believe there is. She chose to take on his burden and attach it to her shoulders and proclaim the worth of a man who had been deemed despicable. She saw desirability when others had chucked him by the wayside. She crawled down in there next to him and stayed put. Or maybe she dragged him out and dusted him off.

Just then, she pointed me to Jesus and all of His promises and to all that He had accomplished.

There she was. The simple act of her making tea for this man made him more than a murderer in my eyes, too. She helped me see him as a husband. As a person capable of giving and receiving love. A person able to be saved by the God-above-all-gods and His son Jesus. Although as different from me as I could imagine, that person might not be as different as it appeared at first glance.

She helped me see beyond. She held so much power as she spoke to me through her silence. Reminding me that love was always bigger.

Was there hope for this man?

Maybe he felt as Eve had felt, as she stood outside of the garden, burying her head in her hands, the hands that had taken what was not hers to take and had ripped her God from her grasp in one tiny, little moment.

Maybe he felt as Adam felt, as he stood outside of the only home he had ever known with no way to get back to the world and the God he had loved.

The shock of that line of before and after blazing before their eyes, across their world and lives and wanting to go back, make a different choice, and have a re-do.

The shock that there was no going back.

But the thing is, even after that moment of complete separation and pain and the entrance of sin and death and evil into the world, God had made a plan to make it all right again.

If the before and after had been reconciled by Jesus in the great story of the Bible, this man's before and after could be reconciled.

There was enough hope for me to see at that moment, and I heard Ethan declare out loud in a kind and gentle voice that he believed there was hope for this man, too. We believed.

The shackles of sin and shame had been shouted at and had collapsed beneath the love above all loves as Jesus gave up His life. Jesus recovered what was lost and handed it back with mercy and grace in His eyes, saying, this is for you. All who are weary. All who are heavy-laden. Come—those who have lied and murdered and stolen. Come. It is not too late. There is freedom. There is love for you.

I was sitting with my knees inches away from this man, remembering he was a murderer, but knowing he was so much more than that, and I saw God's power. God's power had wowed me before with brilliant skies, towering mountains, and raging oceans. But today, his power took my breath away by seeing the second chance it could give to those certain there would be no second chance.

And I knew that God had done the same for me. I hadn't

murdered. But my heart had been full of sin and shame and all kinds of yuck when He called to me. Come. While I was still a sinner, Christ died for me.

While this man was still a sinner, Christ died for him. And for all those out there, suffocated by sin and even those who don't give much or any thought to their sin, Christ died for them, too. Come.

*A Tibetan man spinning a prayer wheel
and thumbing prayer beads*

CHAPTER 21

*A*s we left the home of the man with the shriveled hand, we were confronted by police with assault weapons all over the road. Another murderer had escaped from a town a few hours down the road, and they thought he had tried to dodge authorities by hunkering down in our little mountain village.

It always felt like too much too fast in this simple-looking but complicated place. There was so much happening externally that I couldn't keep up internally. Every time I was shocked by something, another shocker would greet me from behind before I could recover from the first.

We were coming up on our first marriage anniversary. I'd kept a list of all the different places we'd slept over the past year. There were fifty-two different places that we'd laid our heads down over that year. That was one a week. And I was feeling it. The transition was taking its toll, and I was ready to admit it by saying it aloud.

That line between feeling tired and feeling too tired seemed blurry, but I was pretty sure I was crossing it. Over lunch, I told Ethan that I was so relieved that we didn't have to get in a car and would be sleeping in our "own" beds that night, the ones we were currently renting at ShiDa's guesthouse.

But ironically, we did not end up sleeping in those beds that I was so desperately counting on. Instead, in another shocking yet predictable turn of events, we drove four hours to try to outrun danger and escape tragedy and added bed number fifty-three to our growing list.

It started as a work dispute between the road construction workers. One man punched another man for some reason, and tensions grew. Racial friction and hostility were major issues in this part of the country, and things tended to flare up quite quickly when different ethnic groups were involved. This incident was no different.

A stabbing was close behind the punches, and then the mob grew. Three hundred people fighting. The police just ran.

I was supposed to meet Ethan at three o'clock, on the other side of the bridge in town. As I made my way there, the scene unfolded right before my eyes. Men whooping and hollering, picking up stones and shovels, and charging. I instinctively turned and ran. The verse we had just memorized flowed out of my lips as I ran, "The Lord is on my side as my helper. I will not fear." I said it repeatedly to soothe my jiggling legs as I looked for safety.

I found an older woman and man I knew huddled in their little shop, and they welcomed me in. My fear was palpable, and the tears worked their way down my cheeks. The older man laughed, and his wife tried to make light of the situation we found ourselves in, while my heart pounded in my ears.

Before it began, Ethan was at the top of the hill overlooking the town with a Tibetan man, deep in conversation. Unfortunately, he had a front-row seat to what would later be referred to as the riot. He'd never seen such violence—people beating each other with stones, metal bars, wooden planks. At least four cars were destroyed in anger, smashed, and flipped on their sides.

We always hear about and talk about and experience the tension between races here, but seeing it so violent close up did something deep inside us. In this tiny town, the unrest seemed amplified. Reconciliation seemed impossible.

How much grace and forgiveness would it take to transform this society? Right now, it seemed like more than was available.

As soon as the brutality calmed down, Ethan was able to make his way across the bridge to look for me. I was on the lookout for him, and it wasn't too hard to make contact in a town with only one street.

He was visibly shaken in a way I had never seen before, and his concern for my safety had grown as he had watched smoke billowing into the sky from town. He knew I was somewhere in the heart of that, but he had no way to cross over the bridge that had been transformed into a battleground.

As the city smoldered, we checked in with our leaders by phone, who advised us to lay low for a few days in a town a few hours down the road while we watched what was to come in Jangka before deciding if it was safe to return again or not.

Tensions seeped over into the following days when a truck

killed three children and then refused to pay for the hospital bills that mounted up as the doctors had worked to save them to no avail. Fights broke out in the street over minor scuffles that had to do with sales but probably had their start from something more lying just under the surface. We heard that a man had been taken to a hospital a few hours down the road but would never make it back to join the living in his home.

Our hearts broke for the people who had endured the worst of it, and at the same time, we were having trouble putting ourselves back into a place where it seemed anything was possible. Horrible things were possible. We tried to separate the event from the place that we loved and made our way to our room at ShiDa's after several days.

Heading back into town for the first time afterward felt hard. Scary. Almost traumatic. Even though it looked the same as before the riot, the place had changed for us. Everything had been cleaned up. Life was back to normal, showing no visible reminders of the violence that had just consumed the place. But for us, everything had changed. A place of nostalgia had turned into a place of horror for a brief period, and our brains were having trouble switching back to remembering it as a sweet mountain town.

Those we knew closely talked about what had happened, but usually only to point out that Ethan and I had no heart, no courage, and we were cowards for leaving. The guilt was intense, but didn't our safety matter, too? I can only speak from my own experience and from the stories I have heard from others whose paths we crossed over our years in China. Still, a lot of us carry a certain degree of mental health struggles to this day that was either begun or triggered by events we experienced in that place. Multiple people have been diagnosed with PTSD. I have remnants of incidents that I haul with me every day, causing my heart to race and my breath to quicken at seemingly random events that generate my fight or flight response system.

That system was full-fledged working in the weeks after this ordeal. A Tibetan man letting out a whoop within earshot would cause me to panic and look for a place to hide. I was on edge. Ethan was too.

We also learned quickly that while this riot was a significant occurrence, it wasn't unique. Fighting was as commonplace here as the motorcycles rapidly replacing the horses as the primary mode of transportation.

I came to see Jangka as a town in what I pictured as the wild west. It was a bit lawless and scrappy, with death always lurking around the corner and then too visible when it arrived.

We had to adjust to this fragility of life, and it took a significant amount of energy to tote around on your shoulders every day.

We spent so much of our overseas career looking for the chance to get to live directly among the people. Having to wade through doubt about if you even have what it takes once you get there is a very strange and concerning feeling. We were not expecting that.

It's not things you usually anticipate that get you down in the end. To me, the apparent hurdles were physical. Staying warm, options for bathing, avoiding sickness, and leaving behind any semblance of comfort. But in experience, the mental strain, the emotional stress, and the uncertainty took so much more of a toll than I ever predicted.

My body went into overdrive, trying to anticipate any hazard or emergency that might strike at any time. Watching crises unfold in others had a similar effect on me as if it was happening to me. Because life was lived in a constant state of stress, I began to obsess over the things I could control. I was always on guard, trying to make life as stable as possible, working out all of the little things within my power, hoping that the outside circumstances would cooperate.

But they didn't. They never did.

I started trying to figure out how I could surrender the idea of stability while still keeping my sanity because I reached a breaking point while trying to carry that burden in the way I was. I was exhausted by bracing for whatever chaos threatened to consume me next.

I was convinced there was no way to keep to any schedule out here, even though I was craving that more than anything. So, to combat this unpleasant feeling, I did the next best thing and instead called my plan a routine. Although a tiny shift in perspective, this gave me some level of stability I was desperate for, but inwardly helped me prepare for flexibility.

A routine felt less stringent than a schedule, never plugging in specific times for specific things, but instead gave me something to follow while also not falling apart when that routine would be interrupted. And it would be interrupted. Regularly. I knew I had to get myself to a place where I could let life roll over me as it willed.

There was no other way to survive out here.

Each morning, I would make the one-mile walk into the town center. As I passed the cabbage harvesters in their fields, I would pray Psalm 37. "I will choose to delight IN THE LORD. I will commit my way TO HIM. I will trust HIM. I will rest in HIM. And I will wait for HIM." And I would ask for the strength I needed to do it.

Then I put one foot in front of the other, often crossing the street multiple times to avoid the street dogs.

In the words of Elizabeth Elliot, I "did the next, right thing."

I reminded myself that this day was the only one I had right then. And it was the only one I would need to get through. I didn't need to worry about strength for the next month or year—only one day. I lived day by day because that was all that felt possible to me.

It also forced me to be present, fully present, which I realize was maybe one of the most precious gifts of all.

I also made measurable goals. How many hours each week I would practice the language with others or study my books. I had a goal to make five new friends and visit five old friends. I wrote these goals into prayer requests that I kept in my Bible or even in my pocket that could be crossed off when they were accomplished.

I also reflected regularly. I would write a list of everything I had seen God do over the previous month. In the day-to-day, it was harder to see progress. But when I took a chunk of time and looked back, I was encouraged, and my faith was bolstered. It made me motivated to push forward.

It's easy to have a tendency to think of all of the things that need doing. The list is always long, and it usually never gets any shorter. Overwhelm and discouragement can set in too quickly, even if that's not a very accurate picture of how things stand. Celebrating what had already been accomplished helped shift my mindset and fueled my fire.

While these things were helpful, just a couple of months into our life in Jangka, I felt like the amount of giving this life required was hard to supply. Isaiah 58 says, "If you pour yourself out for the needy, you'll be a well-watered garden." I was pouring myself out. Of that, I was sure. But I felt like soon there would be nothing left. I certainly didn't feel like a well-watered garden.

Where did that leave me?

I wasn't sure.

The kicker for me was that I could see Ethan felt the same way as I did. He was bone-deep tired.

We prayed the verse that encouraged us not to grow weary in doing good and promised that we would reap if we did not give up. But we were weary. So weary.

The Bible promised that His presence would go with us and give us rest, but we could not find rest that felt like it was enough. We were teetering on the brink of something, and that something felt not good. I worried that we were near a tipping point. I could see it written all over Ethan's face, too.

And that scared the socks off of me.

The thing that feels hard to describe is the good that we

experienced amidst all of this hard. In many ways, these months were some of the hardest of our lives and some of the best. The joy that rubbed up against the misery was unparalleled. We did feel God's hand supporting us, always just enough, even as our strength withered. We knew beyond a shadow of a doubt that we were in the right place and the satisfaction from that is a remarkable thing. We had genuine delight in our relationships and in the scenery, and in the lifestyle we got to live for that season. We knew it was a gift, and it felt like a gift, even in the trenches. Most people describe joy and sorrow somehow like that, it seems. When one is extreme, the other often is too. Would I take the extreme hard for the extreme good?

I think my answer to that is yes.

Just when I thought there was nothing left, it seemed like God added just enough gas to the tank to keep us scooting on down the road.

CHAPTER 22

*P*eople always ask us what food we miss most when in China and away from America. I'm not sure the most accurate answer to that question, but I can tell you that at the end of a trip to the US of A, we made a special trip to the grocery store to carefully select a delicacy we would not see for a few more years. I picked a bag of tortillas chips and avocados to make guacamole. Ethan picked sausage.

Hands down, the thing I missed most about America, not including people, of course, was central heat. We wore long underwear for at least five months out of the year and wore down coats inside the house over multiple layers, and I still never really felt comfortable. Showering during the cold months was misery, stripping down in rooms where you could see your breath and trying to let the warm water heat you back up, only to step back out into Jack Frost's clutches while you raced to layer up and dry your hair.

In the beginning, going back and forth between China and America, even though it wasn't very often, felt like whiplash. I remember simple things like carpet under my feet while sitting in an overstuffed leather recliner was enough to distract me from whatever was happening around me and basically rendered me speechless. It felt bizarre, even though I had grown up and lived most of my life in this exact locale.

It just seemed strange that people lived with whole yards of spaces to themselves and dishwashers and dryers and multiple cars while a whole lot of the world lived crammed into tiny rooms with nothing more than the barest of bare necessities.

Once, a day after I stepped from Asian life into American life, I was at a bridal shower. It was so shocking to me to see the massive piles of gifts, wrapped in shiny paper with shiny bows, all things the bride herself had picked out and input into a computer, and then other people went and paid for them and handed them over. There was no way I'd tell my friends on the other side of the world about this tradition.

Over time, it got easier to trade in our forks for chopsticks and return the car we'd borrowed to hop back onto our one-speed bikes. We got good at enjoying luxury when we had it and being content without it when we didn't.

The one thing that only seemed to get more complicated over the years was figuring out our identity. We weren't Chinese, even though that was the culture and society we spent most of our time in. We learned how to be adults there, paying our bills at the bank, knowing where the guys who could fix bikes hung out, and navigating the bureaucracy and paperwork needed to conduct our business as residents of China.

We also weren't Tibetan, as much as we tried to make our

lifestyle and persons relatable to them. We could easily move among them, converse deeply, and understand expectations, but some things always separated us. Like resources. As much as we pretended we were just one of them, both of us always knew that we could purchase a plane ticket and be gone at any given moment, slipping back into a lifestyle that would be shockingly lavish to most of an entire nationality.

I would never completely be able to shake off my foreignness, although I certainly did try many times and in many ways. I kept my hair long and wore clothing that was similar to theirs. To the best of my ability, I tried to avoid cultural taboos and add their cultural ways of being into who I was and how I responded and acted. I did want to become all things to all people like the apostle Paul, that I might win some for the sake of the gospel.

But I had my American upbringing hanging on my insides, as was evidenced when, with no shame, I'd stop off in an American restaurant and sink my teeth into a juicy hamburger and fries and milkshake before I even opened the front door of my apartment after a long trip to the mountainside.

In our city apartment, I'd regularly cook up American-like food in my very Chinese apartment, going to great lengths to make lasagna noodles from scratch, homemade sauce, and purchasing cheese from an American restaurant in town.

Yes, I was American. But yet, I felt like a faux American when I landed in America proper. I had difficulty connecting with the topics that seemed to interest everyone else, if I even knew what they were talking about. TV shows, movies, music, and pop culture had become a completely foreign language to me, and I couldn't care less. Some of the hot topics in the church also seemed unrelatable to me, like how it was important to say Merry Christmas instead of Happy Holidays to show your loyalty to Jesus. Was that really it?

Simple tasks in America felt foreign, and we still laugh about the time we tried to go through a McDonald's drive-through. After ordering, they told us to pull up to window number one, and after a quick and stressful conversation between the two of us, we decided window number one must be the one at the very front. As we pulled all the way forward and the cars inched in behind us, we eventually were greeted by a very confused teenage worker rapping at our window, holding out a bag and saying they couldn't find us. It turns out window number one had been the next one in succession, not the one at the end of the line, and we had missed paying and getting our food altogether. We filed that skill away in our brains for the next time we might need it.

You always need to have close to exact change when you purchase something in China. Most people would not accept the equivalent of a twenty-dollar bill for something that cost five dollars. Ethan had to give me a nudge when I explained to the cashier at a gas station that I only had big money, but I wanted to get a drink, and was that okay?

We had become adults in China and had never learned some simple ways to adult back in America.

One way that allowed the two worlds to collide was when a Tibetan family we knew either in America or Tibet had family on the other side of the pond and would ask us to visit or take packages back and forth. Surprisingly, this became a regular part of my life.

One time, I was given a heavy package by some Tibetans in the US to carry back to their relatives I had never met in a very remote and seemingly mysterious Tibetan village. Getting in touch with people out here was very different from anything we were used to. Many people didn't have phones, and the ones who did seemed to change their phone number as much as they changed their socks, which felt like a complete misuse of the phone's very function. So the only way to get in touch with most of them was to physically try to find their exact location at that moment in the world itself.

Maps don't mean a thing out here, and when your whole world is encased in what is between the mountains of your hometown, anything else is not even comprehensible. I had brought my sister back with me for a visit to my Chinese home, and I left her to guard the bags. At the same time, I ran around in a steady drizzle, sticking my head in various car windows to ask the driver if they would be passing by anywhere near our desired destination and could give us a lift.

After many negatives, I found a man willing to go, but we would have to wait to fill up his van with other passengers. As the search began, we ordered some spicy grilled potatoes from a vendor on the side of the road. An hour later, we had our traveling companions, and just before takeoff, two more jumped in, along with a twenty-five-pound bag of roasted barley flour and a massive sack of raw meat.

A few miles out of town, we stopped again for gasoline. No,

not just in the tank, but in three massive containers that somehow managed to fit somewhere in this circus clown car.

Back on the road, a passenger lit up a cigarette, and my sister looked at me with fear in her eyes. I tried to play it cool, although, granted, we had about 400 gallons of gasoline in the back of the car. They all assured us our worry was ridiculous.

After a while, the conversation lulled, and it was time to start looking for some road trip entertainment. Ah yes, it was time for the circle sing. One by one, we were all asked to sing a song. Of course, there was a ten-minute squabble between each song where the desired singer would say, "but I don't know how to sing, I can't, I'm too embarrassed." All of us would say, "yes, you can, come on," The person finally begins and starts belting out with no nerves whatsoever like they are on a Broadway stage.

When it was my turn, I sang "Swing Low, Sweet Chariot." Why? I have no idea; it was just the first song I thought of. We had such a good time that it was decided we'd have another round.

What would I sing this time? A week before, I had just participated in a Tibetan song workshop. I decided to give one of the new songs I had learned a try, even though my confidence in my ability was low to get the words out just right.

I pulled out my song sheets and started singing in Tibetan. "What a wonderful, joyous new day that God has given to us. I want to thank and praise Him. He has loved me. He has taken away my sin and made me right. Thank you, Jesus."

When I stopped singing, they were all talking, saying, "What song is that?" The monk in the front seat (they always got the front seat) grabbed the song sheet from my hand as the token reader in the car and started reading the lyrics aloud to everyone. Even from the mouths of monks, God's word can be spoken.

We arrived at our destination. And by arrive, I mean we were kind of sort of hopefully close. We started asking anyone we saw if they knew where so and so lived. Eventually, we were told to wait, and at some point, two motorbikes screeched to a halt in front of us, and we were directed to get on. My sister had been a trooper, and I wondered what my mom would think if she knew her two daughters were currently on the back of motorbikes with men being driven to an unknown destination in the middle of the Tibetan plateau.

But they took us to the relatives we were looking for. Seriously. It felt like an actual miracle. Maybe it was? I will say it was one of the most incredible things ever to get to provide that link and witness its unfolding firsthand.

It's so interesting to see someone look so similar to someone else that you've only known in a particular context. Doma in the US was a nurse and had kids in suburban elementary schools. Her sister, who was the spitting image of her, lived way up in the mountains and worked in fields and herded yaks in Tibet.

Getting in touch with people worked the other way, too. Instead of working hard to make connections, sometimes they would accidentally fall into our laps! So often, we'd be walking down some random road, not in our city and not in their town, and we'd cross paths with a random friend. It was bizarre how often this happened, and it almost felt like we could come to expect it. It was a much smaller world out there and kind of felt like running into people at the grocery store in a small town back in America.

One time, we specifically tracked down a good friend of mine who had been living in the city but was back with her family in their mountain home. When we arrived, I was pretty excited. How many hours had she spent sitting at my table or on my couch during her first semester of University? And now, here I was, getting to experience her home for the first time.

Her home was clean and fresh and lit up with natural light. Her younger sister took on the bulk of the responsibility and was the complete opposite of her sister in both her physical appearance and her chosen lot in life. My friend was long and lean and looked like she could dance across a ballet stage at any moment by her natural, graceful movements and the way she carried herself. Her sister was strong and heavyset and built for farm work.

Her sister had been married at the ripe old age of fourteen to another fourteen-year-old as the family tried to stay afloat after the death of the mother. They needed to bring a man into their home, which is not the norm, but with only two daughters and now no mother, they needed to figure things out.

As we heard more of their story, Ethan exclaimed, "I was there! I was at your wedding!" Someone he had been staying with had taken him to what had felt like a very random wedding a couple of years back, and here we were, sitting in the bride's living room.

We had great joy in bringing small gifts with us as we visited homes.

The suitcases that I would bring back and forth from the US

and China were usually filled with small gifts. We'd buy T-shirts and hats and pocket knives and make-up and jewelry to give to Tibetan friends. We'd often pick out things with specific people in mind. I remember bringing a small, wooden, model kit of a house for a young nomad girl, and the hours we spent together constructing it and the knowledge that it was one of her first-ever toys were very special.

And we remember the gifts given to us: traditional clothing, heavy earrings, tea, and fruit.

One family spent two days on a bus with the raw leg of a yak held the whole way on their lap to present to us upon their arrival.

Now that feels a whole lot like love to me.

CHAPTER 23

I started noticing that I was getting much more comfortable talking about religious matters in Tibetan. Life out in the village required complete immersion into the language, and my brain had slowly been working with me to make the transition. One thing I wasn't planning on was how much I struggled with comparing myself to my dear husband Ethan, which was why I suddenly found myself spending most of my days alone.

Ethan had been a catch, that was for sure, and I regularly found myself pondering how I was the one who got to end up with him with so many other fish in the great sea of the world. He was a gem of a human being, and he was a wonderful husband. Our relationship could only have been described as pure bliss in our first year of marriage. So many people had told me to expect a rocky start after getting married at a slightly older age than average and that the first year of marriage was often the hardest. That was not to be. He was gentle and caring and kind and fun. And I hoped I was, too.

I reveled in having breakfast with him every day and loved that our work allowed us rarely to be separated during the daytime. We were good friends, good companions, two peas in a pod, and we were in puppy-dog love. Our honeymoon stage lasted way beyond our honeymoon. We never seemed to need space from each other, and everything seemed smooth as silk.

But then something drove the smallest wedge between us, and I almost fell apart. It was my own doing, for I sought out things that appeared to confirm some deep-seated lies that I continued to hang on to, long after being permitted to be freed from them.

Here's what happened. I had never been shy about speaking my broken and emerging Tibetan. I am not a perfectionist, and I never struggled with needing to get it right when talking in a second language. Communication of some sort was always the only thing I cared about. I didn't give enough time or effort to perfect the sounds, which was demonstrated after I had received my first Chinese assessment, only months after arriving in the country. While scoring reasonably high, I was told that my Chinese was "taxing" to listen to in no uncertain terms. I wasn't too bothered. I was a talker in English and Chinese, and Tibetan. I liked to talk any way that was available, mistakes and all.

But as Ethan and I got deeper and deeper into functioning in the Tibetan language, I started to clam up. I was so self-conscious. My husband *was* a perfectionist. He said everything right all of the time. And I never said anything perfectly suitable, and I think I had a thick accent that I wasn't trying too hard to lose.

Furthermore, he not only had studied two-and-a-half years

more than me, but he was also a very fast learner. Again in his favor, he learned best by listening and could catch on to phrases Tibetans used in casual conversations and hung on to them strongly enough to sneak them into the next conversation we would have. And he could turn on the personality! My reserved, quiet, cool-as-a-cucumber husband became the life of the party in Tibetan.

He had corrected my language several times, just being helpful, as he would want someone to do that for him.

But I did not.

It made me feel inferior and nervous and not quite good enough and more than happy to take a back seat, albeit resentfully. So, I shut my lips. Not that it was all that much my choice anyway, because I found that when I was not the center of the conversation as I had become accustomed to being, the conversation moved too quickly for me, and there I was splayed out in the dust. The worst part was that no one seemed to notice.

Sometimes I missed enough that I didn't even know what they were talking about. Sometimes, just as I knew what was happening and had something to contribute, they moved on before I could get out the words.

Tibetans are also very free about stating the obvious truths of life, one of which was that Ethan's Tibetan was so much better than mine. Oh, how many times had I heard those words! Each time they pounded me down, just a little bit, and soon I didn't even feel able to stand up anymore. I just gave up.

It's easy to neglect how far you've come when all of a sudden, you're faced with how far you have to go.

I came up with so many reasons why it didn't even matter that I was there. I felt like a bump on a log that was easily tolerated but not useful. It began to eat at my very center of worth and value.

I was embarrassed that Ethan had chosen a wife like me, and now he was stuck. I initially thought I had been a great choice. I was a go-getter and had made solid strides as a single cross-cultural minister of the gospel, and I thought had so much to offer a seasoned global worker as a partner, a teammate. But now I saw the truth: I was only great when I compared myself to nothing. When compared to something better, well, I pretty much just disappeared.

My underlying fear of not being good enough had now taken center stage, and I was ready to shut this play down so I didn't have to stare at it every day.

Somewhere along the way, I had latched on to the idea that my worth was directly connected to what I could offer or what I produced. Out here, I was starting to feel like I wasn't offering or producing anything when I sat next to Ethan.

So my obvious solution was not to sit next to him.

I started to spend my days mostly on my own. After breakfast, I left in the morning and had my own routes through town, my own relationships developed in my way and with my own talking. I tricked myself into feeling successful and competent, and Ethan and I discussed how beneficial this arrangement could be. To his credit, I'm pretty sure he was oblivious to the fire raging in my soul.

This, of course, left matters unsettled, and it was not the

correct solution, but it seemed to soften and ease the sharp, invisible prongs that were poking into my flesh from every direction, and life felt bearable to me.

Also, in all fairness, with the help of hindsight, there were a few silver linings to this situation, ones which should be noted when creating a more comprehensive plan for engaging in this type of work.

I was forced to use my language and keep up while not struggling to find my footing in a game I was unprepared to play. My language grew, and I could have highly intimate conversations with women about birth control, forced sterilizations, abortion, marriage, and childbirth, all things that never would have happened with a man standing there. It was more natural in many situations. Conversations moved inward, more authentic, and more meaningful to them and me.

But it left the more profound matters of my wounded heart untouched. It let the sadness sit there and fester and strangle me slowly.

It boiled down to that same old desire of all humanity of wanting to be accepted, just as I was.

I wanted to be enough, just as I was.

The thing that is so peculiar about this whole situation is that I had very recently had such a big revelation with the noodle sister with a toothache just weeks earlier. I had found it easy to accept who she was at that very moment, but I was having a much harder time offering that to myself.

The battle raged on and on and on.

I was determined to believe that I was perpetually lacking

in something. I had this unnatural craving to put myself down, to stare at my weaknesses while minimizing my strengths. I was always looking forward, trying to work toward the me that would finally be right, and disregarding the me that stood there, in that day, as not desirable or deserving.

I wanted to be known, and I wanted to be loved. It was painful for me to watch everyone knowing Ethan and loving Ethan, and I felt like I would never measure up.

Funny enough, now I can see that I was already wanted. I was already enough, but no one could convince me otherwise. I was the only one delivering the verdict that I was not adequate or acceptable just as I was. My ears strained to hear that I was worthwhile or valuable, but whether those words were whispered or shouted, they swirled in the air around me and refused to go in.

Having been married for over a decade, I know Ethan well enough to know that when he tells me anything, I can trust his words to mean exactly what they say. Nothing more, nothing less. I've tried over the years to attach a hidden meaning to his words, which I've learned is one of the only things that will get him riled up. His words are chosen with care and precision, and they're accurate. Don't mess around with them.

When he spoke words of life over me, declaring me, myself, his joy, it was strictly the truth. He never wavered in the value he put on me, and he told me point blank he didn't care what I did or didn't do or could or couldn't do because it was me, the me that was right there, that he wanted.

And God was like that, too. All of the words written in His Bible were words I could take at face value. No hidden agenda.

They were not promised for one day when I finally hit the mark or did everything right. His love, care, and joy for me were available and consistent, and straightforward.

No strings attached. I could relax in his love. Not with the good and bad separated into piles, but mixed together in a big lump, tangled and intertwined and accepted.

And I think the Tibetans liked me too. I think they did want me. My language being inferior to Ethan's was just a fact floating in the great big sea of all of the other facts and had nothing at all to do with how they felt about me as an individual. It wasn't bad; it wasn't good; it just was. The same way their care for me just was. The same way Ethan's love for me just was. The same way God's joy in me just was.

Here's the kicker. The world needed me just as I was during that time.

Looking back, I can see some of the specifics now. Things I would never have considered strengths or gifts or notable were incredibly important to the people around me and our situation.

Ethan's list of gifts looked long and strong when I looked at him. They seemed like heavy hitters for the tasks that we were regularly faced with. He was smart, good at languages, and physically cut out for this harsh climate and situations. He could be counted on to make steady progress in absolutely whatever he set out to do. He was consistent and a hard worker.

I, on the other hand, was impulsive. At first glance, that may seem like a less than desirable characteristic. BUT. When you paired it together with Ethan's analytic, methodical way of decision making, it came in more than handy to get the ball rolling when it needed rolling. I was much more likely than he was to try something new, which opened most of the doors we ultimately walked through.

I was a dreamer. While Ethan's careful, deliberate, and realistic approach to life helped rein me in a bit, I provided the optimism that he and I needed when the going got tough. I could see the big picture, see beyond, and I believed that anything was possible.

I was friendly, approachable, and an extrovert, making and maintaining friendships with ease. I wanted to know everyone, which led us to be exposed to a wide array of people from various walks of life. It gave us a fuller picture of this place and the people.

My life did have an impact. I did have things to offer. Even when I couldn't see it, or even if I wasn't able or willing to acknowledge it, the world was better just because I was in it. Fact.

Yes, I mattered, too.

Cultivating a working life with Ethan was something we had to work on. I mean that it didn't just happen. And I mean that we had to work on it regularly and with a tremendous amount of effort. Ethan had to work on being quiet, which is hilarious since that is *not* his problem in the English-speaking world. And I had to work on speaking up, which is just as hilarious because that was *not* my problem in the English-speaking world. Funny how personalities can almost be altered in foreign lands with foreign words!

We had to communicate clearly with one another about how we were feeling and how we should be feeling and how we could practically change aspects of working together and then practice it and make a mess of it and then cry and then do it all again. We had to learn to celebrate progress over perfection in this area, as it was something that would nip at our heels for, well, forever, as far as I can tell.

CHAPTER 24

*E*than was losing weight. I was worried he was too skinny. His butt hurt when he sat on it, which couldn't be a good sign. Food was pretty limited out there compared to what we were used to. Diarrhea was also a pretty constant companion for us. I was skinny, too, but not like Ethan.

People were starting to comment that we looked unhealthy. I wondered how it could be that this diet and lifestyle were wearing us down to nothing when the people that lived here looked so hearty and healthy. What were we doing wrong?

I was starting to wonder more and more often if this life was sustainable for us. I would feel God's grace and strength filling me up, and then soon after, I would fall, feeble and weak, causing me to doubt our ability to make it physically. The thought felt intrusive, as I didn't want it to be something I had to consider. This was my dream. This was our dream. And it was happening. No line would be too much to cross, right?

It was obvious our bodies were failing us, and I was frantically trying to revive them. We had long ago run out of the

Snickers bars we had carried in on our backs, and calories in never seemed to add up to the calories we expended just walking those mountain roads. I felt unsure how to right the ship.

Mentally and emotionally, things were tough, too. The phones had been blocked due to political unrest. Our security of having a cell phone to connect us to the outside world had been taken from us. There was no way for us to contact anyone outside of the country, but we also couldn't even call down to the city that we considered our home base. It felt like we existed in another reality, and I thought of those who had gone before us long ago, who carried their coffins with them to the field, knowing they'd never see loved ones again. So maybe I was being a bit dramatic, after all, but this state we'd found ourselves in felt quite strange and precarious.

We were very much alone.

One morning, Teacher Sunshine wanted us to go to a particular event with her, and we agreed without really knowing to what we had agreed. She'd be pretty hard to say no to anyway, and I generally loved all of my minutes spent with her. I thought it would be an easy day.

But when we arrived, we realized we'd been put in a very awkward situation. It was an event at a local monastery, a monastery we'd heard all kinds of crazy stories about. Most Tibetans say it's cursed, and you shouldn't even touch any objects that have ever been there, and here we were, ourselves, objects smack dab in the middle of it.

Adding to that, a living Buddha was visiting that day, teaching and blessing the villagers. We felt like we were invading this unique space at precisely the wrong time while feeling like we were on sticky ground ourselves from a spiritual vantage point.

We tested out the words "we'll wait for you" on Teacher Sunshine, and to our surprise, she readily agreed. We made our way to the edge of the compound, only to accidentally stumble into the sky burial area. I had never actually seen one, even though it's one of the first things I had learned about Tibetan Buddhist rituals and practices. A large slab of stone lay waiting to help dispose of the human dead. Designated persons have the duty of crushing the bones and bodies to prepare them to be eaten by vultures and carried away—an actual burial in the sky.

As the realization of where we were dawned on me, I looked up to see giant birds circling above and felt absolutely like running for anywhere but these hills on which we stood. As we bolted, we made our way through the crumbling, white-washed stone buildings and found a small stream on the other side, a much better and more appropriate resting place.

When we saw Teacher Sunshine arriving from a distance after a short time, we were pleased and relieved. We were ready to hightail it out of there and leave this place far behind. But, as we followed her through the narrow mud passageways that wound their way between the simple village homes, we found ourselves only going deeper in.

Her relatives lived here, in this cursed pocket of the valley, and we entered into their very dark home. We had to wait for our eyes to adjust after being in the high-altitude sunlight, and our minds worked frantically to try and work out our next steps.

The so-called cursed-ness of this village came much more

from this segment of society's willingness to submit to the Chinese government's way of doing things than any spiritual element. The Chinese government had appointed the leaders of this monastery, who were under strict instruction to follow and pass along the wishes of the communist party. Tibetans generally had a solid feeling about this set-up, falling on one side of the issue or the other, and would not mix with those standing on the other side of that line. We were feeling even more and more the need to get out of this heated and complicated war ground. This was an area where we would definitely remain neutral.

We welcomed the tea that was given with a smile, but when handed food to eat, we froze, being once again pushed into a hard-to-handle predicament, completely different than the original predicament.

We had committed to fasting one day a week. With such a sporadic schedule, we decided that it would have to be ingrained into whatever happened in our lives on any given Monday. We had committed to this with a group of people, two of whom were sitting with us then, and we felt that it was a commitment we should and needed to honor.

So, we just blurted it out like it was. We were fasting and could not eat any food. We were worried about offending our hosts by not taking their food, but we also felt wrong for announcing this virtue aloud when the Bible says explicitly don't let others know you are fasting; it's between just you and God. It felt like we were on a run of bloopers with no end in sight.

Fasting is a widespread practice among Tibetans, and we were to imminently hear, extremely respected. They had no problem with us not being able to eat with them, and in fact, it opened up a wonderful and intriguing conversation.

In Tibet, fasts are prescribed by lamas, who seem to dictate a lot of Tibetan life. Being told what to do seems to be very welcomed by Tibetans and not seen as a burden or annoyance.

For example, Tibetans love to "MoDa," which is the topic of conversation around the small table today. The concept is quite appealing in certain ways. When you are faced with a decision, you can go to your assigned lama, and they do a series of rituals that probably involve rolling dice and consulting the stars to advise you on what you should do. People seem pleased to go on their way, knowing the right thing to do and just doing it. No matter how that thing turns out in the end, they have the peace of knowing that their decision was the only right one.

I love my freedom as a Christian believer to go directly to God with my cares and anxieties and my requests and petitions. Direct access to the creator of the universe and the creator of me. The thought is at once so powerful and so intimate.

But there are plenty of moments when I wouldn't mind just being told which way was the right way and carrying on. I do seem to waste much energy trying to decipher which path is correct or prescribed, and then often second guess myself once I'm on the way. I have often thought how nice it would be just to know. I think I would do just about anything if I knew it was THE thing.

My heart wants to obey God. But there are so many moments when knowing *how* to obey God isn't obvious. I feel it mostly in big decisions, but this struggle is also wrapped around the small ones.

We have to make choices—all of the time. We have to put one foot in front of the other and move through our moments. How do I know if I'm choosing to move through the right moments or the wrong ones?

Having someone tell me which choice to make would be a welcome relief at certain times. And where exactly is that line, anyway? I don't need to ask God what clothes to wear each day, do I? But if I plan to move countries, I should probably make sure He's in the mix. And what about all of the differently-weighted scenarios in the middle?

There are a lot of clear-cut commands in the Bible. I am thankful for those. And as I've sat and pondered what it means to obey God in many of the grey areas of life, I've come to a conclusion with which I am willing to sit.

Jesus said that the greatest commandment was to love God and the second greatest was to love people. Was obedience as easy as loving God and loving people?

I loved God. I was confident about that.

And I was getting better at loving people.

Loving people mostly seemed to mean shutting my mouth and opening my ears and being present in the moment with another person.

Most of the time, it seemed like this all happened over tea out here.

Was obeying God so simple? I think it might be.

That day, drinking butter tea in that dark room with

strangers, so many missteps and bungles following our every move, I realized that this was the heart of it all. There is power in exchanging snippets of our lives that we will never get back with another person. There is love, grace, and strength given when we witness another's existence and validate their experiences and emotions. And there is power in letting them acknowledge our presence in the world, along with our convictions and questions, declaring tenderly the place God occupies in our stories, even when that story might be confusing or complex or unfinished.

I was again struck that the questions of life all seemed to be the same, no matter where you come from or who you are, or what you know. The worries about our strange surroundings and their implications all seemed to melt away as we listened to the thoughts and cares of this beautiful and significant family, way out here in the middle of nowhere.

When Teacher Sunshine declared we were all spending the night, we decided that was a line we were unwilling to cross as foreigners in an undocumented location and a tenuous one at that, so we walked most of the way home, which was miles. I decided walking must have been the right transportation decision in God's eyes, as there were no other options available to us. (Ha!)

But as I felt the pounds and strength slipping off me, I wondered how long we could last and how this could possibly be the way the plan was supposed to go.

CHAPTER 25

I had been teaching an English course to Teacher Sunshine's 7-year-old son at her request. I enjoyed it quite a lot, and he was picking things up fairly quickly. We sat on the tree stumps by the woodpile outside their home one day and practiced the song *Head, Shoulders, Knees, and Toes.* We couldn't help but laugh a whole lot as he loudly and animatedly called out body parts in his heavy accent and tried to get to the right ones at the right time faster and faster.

As I was getting ready to leave, Teacher Sunshine's dad was sitting cross-legged on the ground in the front yard keeping his eye on a painter they had hired to decorate the windows of their new home. The painter hung precariously on the edge of a sill fifteen feet off the ground as he brushed a layer of white paint under the bright design he had just finished above the window. His pink baseball cap fit snugly on his head backward, holding his long hair out of his eyes as he worked. His Converse-style sneakers had a big white star on each side, and I wondered if he had added that himself.

Teacher Sunshine's dad held a large, spinning prayer wheel, and he proudly told me he was up to 88,000 rotations. He said to me that as the wheel spun round and round, the prayers inscribed on the inside went out to the god with many arms. He had started this count a month ago with the specific goal of obtaining a better rebirth by getting rid of some of his accumulated misdeeds.

He called me over and wanted to talk to me about sin, which I found was a popular conversation topic. I thought about life back in the states and how we often opened conversations with the weather. Maybe sin was the weather conversation of Jangka, or perhaps the rumors of what we had to say were circulating, and curiosity was high.

Teacher Sunshine's dad was concerned that he had too much sin that he needed to make up for and worked on it through various karmic actions. He wanted to know how I worked to atone for my sins. I think he was looking for tips.

I told him that I didn't do anything to work to cover up my past sins. I said to him that my faith in Jesus is what cleared away my sins once and for all and that I didn't believe there was any particular physical action required to counteract my bad deeds specifically. The look he gave me was one of utter dismissal. I'm pretty sure he thought that way of thinking was ridiculous, but he did ask to hear more about how this strange system could work.

It must have been a shocking comment, as the workman himself glanced down, laid aside his paintbrush, and climbed down to sit with us. I was surprised that Teacher Sunshine's dad did not reprimand him to get back to work, but I had no idea what arrangements they had made. Teacher Sunshine's husband also appeared from nowhere and took a seat.

It was easy for us all to start on the same page, agreeing that everyone does things we would classify as bad at times. We also all agreed that those bad things need a way to go away. It was also easy for us all to acknowledge that it was hard to get rid of that sin and that it was hard, if not downright impossible, to make sure our good deeds do outweigh our bad deeds in the end, if that is, in fact, the utmost goal.

So what do we do about the sin that seems to stick to us, no matter how hard we want it off?

In Tibetan Buddhism, you do what Teacher Sunshine's dad does. You spin your wheel. You walk around the monastery. You chant. You work hard and hope it's enough in the end.

As people, we like action. It makes sense. It feels right and good and powerful. It's a tangible way to feel like we're moving forward—a way to feel good about ourselves.

And we do have to work for most things in life. And so, it feels incredibly natural to work to remove our sin, as well.

So when I told them about the God-above-all-gods' Son, Jesus, and how He is the once and for all "sin-removerer", I wasn't surprised by their looks of incredulousness.

It feels too simple and too wrong to rely on someone else's work rather than our own, especially for something this big and with such massive repercussions.

I can understand why they'd instead carry on, slogging it out, trying to make their way there on their own merit.

We asked questions back and forth to clarify how the other belief system worked. We filled in holes and details and expressed doubts.

Having a conversation like this was so satisfying and helpful. To listen to Teacher Sunshine's dad and his son-in-law and the painter, just as they listened to me. Sharing with people. Back and forth and around again. We asked hard questions about the world, and looked at things from someone else's perspective, and heard our own words through someone else's ears and reactions. Scrutinizing what we know to be accurate and making spaces for ideas we might not agree with.

The apostle Paul talked about sharing not just words but also his entire life with the people he served. I liked to think I was working on doing that, too, that this was a genuine labor of love. That I was sincere and honest, trusting boldly in God while living gently among others.

I hoped they could hear that my message was one of compassion and mercy and one that carried promises of new life. A life that was full and good both right now and for all of eternity.

I wondered how it felt to be sitting on the other side of me. To hear these words and take them in. Maybe they weren't even aware that there were different ways of looking at life and death and the beginning and end of time before today. Without access to good roads and ways of travel, they had little influence from other places.

There was great interest to hear of these other ways of thinking, believing, and doing. But as I shared that this good news was definitely for them as well, and more than just a very, very foreign religion, it seemed like this information could not be received in any way, shape, or form. It wasn't even like it was a rejection on their part of this opportunity that now lay before them. It was like a glass wall placed in front of them, with no possibility of penetration. The choice didn't even seem to exist for them.

I don't think they felt it was a negative interaction. I think they enjoyed learning about Christianity, and they were more than curious. I don't think they even knew that others might conceive that they could feel pressure in a situation like this to conform or accept this new way of thinking as their own.

My interactions with others surrounding religion felt like a conversation. A give and take. Teaching. Learning. It was a joy to chat about these things, and it brought us closer together as friends and as fellow humans walking earth's roads.

As I shared the gospel with various people along my way, many parts sounded strange to my ears when they stood alone, especially placed in front of the backdrop of this other world of snow-capped mountains and monks and prostrating pilgrims. The virgin birth, the world's creation in six days, a flood that wiped out the entire earth, a talking donkey. It's hard to share just pieces of God's story when His story is so big and long and wide and deep and in everything and everywhere.

At times I felt concerned about this, about time limitations and only choosing aspects of the Christian faith to explore as they came up in everyday conversations and situations. Fasting, sin, the afterlife, creation. I was concerned about the words I chose to use and how accurately I was expressing myself from a theological point of view, as well as working in a second language that wasn't anywhere close to perfect.

But then I reflected on my own spiritual journey. There were early years when I didn't know much besides the classic Bible stories of Noah's ark and Daniel in the lion's den, and Jonah and the whale. When I prayed the sinner's prayer at the age of five, it was purely out of desperation and to escape the flames of hell I had recently heard about, rather than understanding my sin and its relation to a pure God.

There has to be a starting point for there to be anything that comes after, right?

We're all growing in our knowledge and love and service to God, no matter where we currently stand on our spiritual quest. We're all working stuff out, no matter who we are or where we've come from, or how far up the church's or monastery's ladder we've climbed. Forward movement happens because there is somewhere further down the line to go. We've all lived through a period of having very little information about the religion we were following and have all had times of deeper diving and learning and growing and thinking.

And on this day, as we talked about sin, I also worried about dangling this particular carrot of "easy" forgiveness in front of them...even though they didn't seem inclined to take it! I was leery of sugar coating the gospel or of making God's gifts out to be the priority rather than God himself.

Then again, my journey with God started out with a desire for what God could give me, more than actually caring too much about God Himself. You know, the escaping hell thing.

I pondered on these words, written by a Tibetan believer:

"There is one way of salvation from sin
That way is Jesus
If I come to Him, He'll cleanse my sins
Through this one way
I'll receive a new heart
He'll make my black heart white

There's one way of salvation from death
That way is Jesus
Those who believe in Him
Will receive eternal life
By one way, I'll get to heaven
That way is Jesus

If I believe in Him from my heart
He will take me there
I believe, I believe
Jesus died for me
His precious blood, His precious blood
Saved me from sin."

As we sat in the grass that afternoon, we shared a moment that I am guessing made a difference in each one of our lives. We all learned something. We all sat quietly and listened to someone else. We all turned inward and examined our beliefs and ways of living. We showed respect to each other. We all moved forward.

That day is also seared into my life for the role that painter would have in my life over the coming years. His story impacted my life so much that I still think about him and his family regularly, as I live out my life on American soil so far away from where he is living out his life.

There are small moments in our lives that become huge. And it's only in hindsight that we can see it. If I could have warned him, I would have. But life doesn't come with very many warnings.

CHAPTER 26

*W*e needed to leave the country to renew our visa, so we headed out for the two-day journey back to the city and to the apartment that held more of our possessions and the landlord's small washing machine. Yippee aye oo ki-yay! I'd been washing our clothes by hand out in the back next to the chickens in our Jangka life, and the dirt that naturally accumulated on clothes out here was definitely more than enough to make them stand up by themselves. My perpetually raw and bleeding knuckles were evidence of what a pampered life I'd lived before now.

At first glance, people may view the Jangka community as a poor one. The majority of homes have no sort of indoor plumbing. There is a shower house in town, open on certain days and heated by a man shoveling coal into a big furnace. If you stroll through town in the early morning, you'll see many people out in the street brushing their teeth and squatting to spit in the road. People are well-fed, but on very simple food and with a very limited variety. There are no extras, but the people here are used to simplicity and seem to truly thrive off of it.

We were also forced to live a much simpler life than we had ever lived before in staying out there. Packing up our tiny bags to leave town took just a few moments. I could sling over my shoulder every single item I'd used for the last months.

In many ways, I found it quite freeing to live with so little. So few decisions to be made. You wear the clean pants and make a note to wash the dirty ones. You put on your only shoes every time you leave the room.

Possessions out here were treasured and accounted for. They were purposeful, needed, or brought significant joy. Rooms were never cluttered, and items were well cared for as they were not easily replaceable.

I returned to the city with two physical items I had not arrived with. One of them was a birthday gift from Ethan. When we first set up our makeshift home, he had set a small, wrapped gift on the shelf. He would refer to it regularly, enticing me with a surprise to come. ShiDa also picked it up and looked at it almost daily, speculating about what could be inside.

When my birthday came, Ethan first gifted me with a roasted duck and grapes, two foods that were hard to come by and acquired at a bit of a cost. I was not taking these gifts with me back to the city, as they had been devoured on the spot. The delicate and beautiful watch with a small leather band was brought back on my wrist instead of in a beautifully wrapped package inside Ethan's backpack. Possessions became so much more valuable when so few existed. They were appreciated in an entirely new way.

The second item I was returning with was a set of fake pearls a lady in town had given me. I cried tears when I received them. Yes, I felt cared for in receiving this gift, but the item was possibly what sparked tears and brought healing to me, rather than the motive behind it.

After we were married, a few days before returning to China, I lost the set of pearls I had worn on our wedding day straight off my neck as I walked down a wintery street. While never having been one to care a whole lot about possessions, this event held significant pain for me.

Because of our nomadic lifestyle, we owned very few possessions. We did receive several wedding presents, but they were not things we would be able to bring over to China.

We had people asking if they could have this or that of our very few belongings and hauling them away before our very eyes. Objects often hold memories, which is why I think we struggle to part with things. As I watched my possessions disappear, it felt like a disassembling of my memories, a loss that went beyond the particular item, but a life that I loved that I was sad to see go, even if I was ready for the other life I was heading toward.

So when I lost those wedding pearls, it was after my last possession had walked out the door. I felt like I was standing there naked and saying, here's what's left, which is nothing but me and my last necklace. A possession I can tie to my physical body to ensure it won't be taken. And then, that too was lost.

I think this may seem trivial, but it was a hard moment for me. I had given up so much. It felt cruel that even the last thing had been taken. It was an emptying that helped me surrender completely, but it wasn't without pain and sadness. It caused a reckoning in my soul, a new commitment and resolve to follow Jesus no matter the cost. I relinquished those pearls and laid myself at His altar to do His work in His way.

Then when I was gifted those pearls that summer, so similar to my last possession to go before arriving out here, it felt like God was saying, I haven't forgotten you. I wore that necklace every day as a reminder.

That whole experience out there in Jangka felt, in many ways, like a fast. Literally with food, but also in letting go of so much. Yes, possessions, but also letting go of my ways of life, my language, privacy, entertainment, and my support system. It had rubbed me raw, but I would easily do it all again. It is a powerful thing to be stripped of what feels like absolutely everything except the very essence of who you are and then be forced to look at it face to face, head-on, with no distractions and nothing to hide behind. To acknowledge all that is for what it is. It's a moment worth fighting for, even if it's miserable to get there.

By His favor, He had made my mountain stand strong (Psalm 30:7). He had given me grace for each moment, even when I couldn't see the grace on its way. He had lifted me up from my failings and pointed me back in the right direction. He had whispered to my heart to set Him before me, and because of that, I was not shaken (Psalm 16:8).

We had seen war, and we had seen peace. We had seen heartache, and we had seen triumph. We had been sick, and we had climbed mountains. We had questioned, and we had preached. We had loved, and we had been loved.

On the morning of our departure, we ate spicy tofu and drank butter tea with ShiDa, who was busy planning a trip to come see us in the city. She had never been to the city before, and I was giddy with the thought of getting to introduce her to that new realm.

Not one for sappiness, she ventured out of her comfort zone and revealed to us that she had stayed put in her guesthouse all summer long without going to her main home because she wanted to be near us. I don't think I could have been happier. It felt like we had accomplished something big. Something real.

We had become connected to this place and these people. And they had become connected to us. Our stories had become intertwined, and I never wanted them to untwine.

At first glance, this place, Jangka, seemed like nothing at all. A few homes scattered along a dusty stretch of mountain road. But oh, this place is something. This place is full of mothers, brothers, fathers, daughters, and grandparents.

Now I had seen them. Now I could never unsee them.

And if these people were here, in this tiny little dot of a spot in our own big and huge world, how many other sisters and uncles and friends and babies were scattered in all of the indentations of the world, breathing and sleeping and hoping and building their own castles in their own air?

For a moment, I wanted to meet them all.

What a big world.

What a big and beautiful world.

CHAPTER 27

*T*hat last day in Jangka, I had so little energy that I wondered if I could even make it around to say my goodbyes. The tired feeling had lodged itself so deeply inside of me that it had become almost a normal way to exist, even as it was starting to dictate what I was and was not able to do. Somehow, I had let myself get so used to the feeling that I forgot to be concerned about it.

After returning to the city, the exhaustion was somewhat harder to ignore, and on top of that, I started to develop specific and sharp pain. I knew my body had been under a lot of stress, so I thought I just needed more time to recover. I chalked it up to that and soldiered on. But soon, the pain was severe enough that I decided to see a doctor.

An ultrasound revealed a cyst, which he thought would need to be surgically removed. I had been advised to leave the country to get this procedure done, as the medical care in the part of the country where we were living was not always reliable or necessarily safe. My first thought was not to worry about the actual medical problem but to be concerned about being forced to travel again. I was so depleted that hitting the road for a much-needed medical procedure sounded almost worse than just letting this baby run its course.

But, we hauled ourselves to Thailand, and by some miraculous intervention, the cyst disintegrated with the help of medicine given to me on the day we arrived. We were able to return home virtually unscathed.

With the pain gone, I thought things would slowly or quickly return to normal, but the tiredness was all-encompassing. I couldn't make decisions, and I was still having trouble functioning.

Living a life as an international Christian laborer can be easily misunderstood. We have received many comments in our life by all kinds of people that demonstrate that our work and life were hard to relate to. Understandably. We got to travel for a living to desirable and exotic locations. Working could, at times, consist of drinking tea and chatting with friends for hours. We got paid to study and learn interesting things. I was well aware of these perks, even if some of those perks didn't always feel like perks after a while.

We have borne the brunt of well-meaning comments that sting deeply. We have been told by Christians in America that our life is a permanent vacation. Or Tibetans themselves made comments at times about how lucky we were that we got to play all of the time. That we didn't need jobs. We just had money and got to do what we wanted.

Chinese people also had a hard time understanding us, and

it got even dicier when they heard about our specific interest in Tibetan people and language. One of the first questions we would get asked when we met new people in China was, "Are you a teacher?" I usually felt a bit embarrassed as I responded, "No, a student," because I knew how that conversation would progress. We'd reluctantly correct them when they assumed we were studying Chinese and wait for their flabbergasted, "But why study Tibetan?" Once we got into how *long* we'd been studying, it was hard to deflect their visibly appalled expression at how much I was wasting my life.

These comments didn't roll off my back as I wish they would have, and I felt a desire to defend myself to those who looked on and thought this work was easy. For the sake of all of the other people currently dogging it out on the field, I'll say it loud and clear. It's not easy.

It's hard never to get a break. And what I mean by that is that no matter if you technically take a day off or even a whole week's vacation, you must still function in a completely different language and culture every day. This is no easy feat for the brain and places a distinct layer of tiredness on top of all of the others. It does get easier, but I would say it never got easy for me.

In many places in the world, people's way of scheduling interactions is not the same. We had people dropping by our doorstep regularly unannounced, sometimes staying an hour, sometimes for days. Dropping everything and caring for people took a significant brain shift and caused stress, and even when we were home alone, tucked comfortably in our bed, I always had a little thought in the back of my brain, wondering who and when the next person was going to show up. I never really felt like I was guaranteed alone time, which I desperately needed to recharge.

Not having a geographically-present boss or leader or someone looking over our shoulder was more challenging than it may seem. Setting your own schedule is a responsibility in itself. We didn't have someone telling us what to do, so we had to figure out the best job description for ourselves at any given time and get to work. I am naturally a self-starter, so I would assume that if this task could be arduous for me at times, for those that would rather follow than lead, it could feel completely overwhelming.

From my experience, very few global workers would or could ever take advantage of this situation. If anything, they tend to have the opposite issue and work themselves down to nothing because the job is never done.

A lack of a specific routine is a big struggle for most. A joke went around that said, "the only thing certain over here is that nothing is certain." Because life was so unpredictable and could be different nearly every day, it was hard to settle into a rhythm. Making new decisions day after day could be exhausting, and being thrown into situations unprepared regularly depletes a person.

Home assignment is another misunderstood part of a cross-cultural worker's life and job. It is more often than not looked upon by others as a break for us. And while there is a small amount of truth to that, many hours each week are devoted to preparing speeches or presentations and often sermons. Preparing a thirty-minute public speaking formal talk to an audience and then actually giving said speech eloquently and without evident nerves is no laughing matter for the bulk of us.

I think I always felt pressure to be happy and helpful. I felt like it was my job to be likable and do whatever I could to help a person out, even if it wasn't even in their best interest. I expended a lot of energy trying to be whatever I thought that person wanted me to be.

Over time, these things weighed on me so heavily that I had trouble sneaking out from under them. After we returned from Thailand after removing my cyst, and the tiredness didn't let up, we had nowhere else to shove the elephant in the room.

We were running ourselves into the ground.

It strikes me as odd that a lifestyle that can give the impression of ease from the outside looking in can wreck you from the inside out fairly quickly.

We needed rest, and we were about to be handed it in a very unexpected way.

Right before we had left Jangka, we talked and had tea with a cousin of ShiDa's who had come for a visit. He had many questions about our beliefs, and as he left, we were able to give him a Jesus film in a sister dialect to his own. He was very excited, and it got us thinking about this little town that had taken up such a prominent place in our hearts.

Jangka had almost nothing to offer in the way of entertainment. A few tea shops were to be found, which offered a place for card playing and possibly some other shady things. A few pool tables lined a corner, and a game could be had for a minimal cost. There were endless rolling hills to walk through and picnic on, but that seemed too much like daily living and taking the animals out to pasture to be considered an exciting option. TVs were plentiful, but the sporadic electricity made it an interesting pursuit. When they could tune in, there was no Tibetan language station, making it impossible for the majority to understand, although it did not stop them from watching the moving pictures. Alcohol flowed freely, and we heard prostitution was pretty rampant. Most could not read, and even if they could, books were limited, and language dialect differences made it almost impossible.

After living the Jangka life ourselves, we took up some of the local pastimes. Staring out of the window for long periods of time and announcing to others if a cow was meandering by. Noting the trucks that would rumble through every great once in a while.

We got particularly excited about this lack of entertainment because Ethan had been asked to help with a project that hoped to see a two-hour movie translated into several different local Tibetan dialects. This movie would span across time from creation to the present day, talking about the God-of-all-gods' place and work in the world. It would follow the story of a Tibetan family while weaving the gospel story throughout, using Tibetan art, dancing, and music.

We felt that if a movie were done in their dialect, many people would clamor to watch it. It would be possibly the first time they could understand the words spoken on the screen. It would also most likely be the first time many of them had ever heard the Good News.

I started crying when Ethan told me about this opportunity. Translation had always been an interest for us, and here he was, ready and able to do the hard work!

Desk work permitted us to rest our minds and bodies from what we had experienced. It allowed routine, simplicity, and order, all things that would do us a lot of good at this stage in our married life.

It also felt like another culmination of a dream. We had studied for years to be able to get to this point. It was hard work learning a language with so few materials available and whose dialects were so widely varied.

Ethan had some previous translation experience when he put together a textbook for our university to aid in beginning studies of the Jangka dialect. It was the first book of its kind and a project he had completed with lots of joy. He hoped it would help others that came behind him learn this unique and challenging dialect that he had needed to learn without the help of a book. That project was satisfying enough that he was ready for a bigger translation project.

It was an easy yes for us.

That initial project rolled into another and another. He had found solid translation partners to work with from the Jangka area. It was highly satisfying work, and it also provided so many profound insights into the culture. Needing to work with non-believers and people unfamiliar with the tenets of Christianity (because none of those people existed) allowed him to see the Scriptures through the lens of people utterly unfamiliar with them.

For example, Buddhism teaches that each person is responsible for working at freeing their own heart from sin because there is no Savior or person to help you. In light of that view, the following error concerning the concept of "forgiveness" came about. The original document said, "if we confess our sin, repent from the bottom of our hearts and turn away from sin, God will truly forgive us." The translation partner's words read, "if we confess our sin, repent from the bottom of our hearts, and destroy and remove our own sins, then God will truly forgive us." This seemingly small difference showed a fundamental misunderstanding of Biblical forgiveness and how people can truly know God.

Wrestling through these concepts didn't provoke tension but instead built camaraderie and a deep partnership as they explored the big questions of life together. The nitty-gritty desk work of picking through a massive pile of words and analyzing them mixed with the meaningful conversation and relationships with translation helpers was a perfect fit for Ethan.

One day, a translation helper looked up from his work and said, "The question before every person is this, do you or don't you believe that Jesus has the authority to forgive sins?"

And that's exactly it, isn't it? It was amazing to watch God's word speak for itself and the lightbulb moments for those looking at it for the first time.

Sometimes the profound things they said seemed to lead away from Jesus, which was hard. One day, a helper said, "Everyone is sick. Their hearts are sick. We all need medicine, and that's religion. But every sickness is different, and each sickness needs different medicine." This seemed to be a very Buddhist view-point that all religions are good and okay and can help you meet your struggles in their unique but beneficial way. It definitely helped us understand their worldview a bit more.

When we gave ourselves so thoroughly to language learning for so many years, our main reasoning was that we wanted to be able to comfortably talk about the Bible in the heart language of the people. We knew that this particular language dialect was largely forgotten and isolated, and our hearts desired to show these people that they had value and mattered. They mattered to us, but even more to the God-above-all-gods. We felt like speaking their language showed them love, care, and respect and communicated that they were important and significant.

But this skill of speaking and writing and reading their language was now being used in another way. We counted thirty-nine people from Jangka that we knew had been exposed to some Biblical truth over three months. Although this was something we rejoiced over, we were struck with the fact that at this rate, it would take 7,819 years for all of this group even to hear just a bit of the good news!

We continued to think about the possible impact of these projects on the areas they were made for, and it seemed huge. We were very aware that there was not a single resource available for people in this area. Nothing. They didn't even have a way to get this information, even if they were looking for it. And, of course, they didn't even know that there was anything to look for.

This translation work would be used to clearly articulate the gospel message in materials that could be shared with a larger audience for many years to come. It could also be used by people who could not speak the people's heart language. To me, it felt like a fantastic legacy to be able to leave behind. Something concrete and permanent to be left behind for Tibetans regardless of where we physically were or were not. Something that would outlast us for years and years to come.

We got encouragement just often enough to keep us going and confident enough in our path. When one project was completed and recorded, it was played for speakers of the Jangka dialect. The results were so encouraging that we cried. A woman in her fifties said her favorite part is the precious Savior. She goes on, "When the Buddhist teachers come in the winter, there are so many people (that attend) that you often can't hear (the teachers) clearly, and sometimes they don't speak an understandable dialect of Tibetan. This is very good Tibetan. If you listen to it (as a foreigner), you'll learn Tibetan very quickly. You should listen to it every night before you go to sleep, and then you won't be lonely or scared." She asked where the carrier got it, and when she was told a friend had given it to her, she said, "You must have a very good friend if they gave you something like that."

We felt like this feedback was more than we could have asked for. The gospel was clearly articulated. It was understandable to those for whom it was written. It left people with a feeling of hope.

Translation felt like not just a good use of time but the best use of time.

CHAPTER 28

One evening, Ethan answered the ringing phone with the Chinese greeting, "Wei!" The person on the other end was having a giggle fit and couldn't seem to get it together enough to respond to Ethan's numerous repetitions of "Who is this?"

Finally, a timid voice said, "Is this big brother noble-minded moon?" Noble-minded moon was the name Tibetans used when they referred to Ethan.

"Yes," he replied, "Who are you?"

"My relative told me to call you if I needed any help once I got to the city."

And so began our introductions to numerous new students from Jangka who had been sent to the city for university after producing high-enough test scores.

It was mind-boggling to me.

Even though we weren't physically in Jangka, God was bringing Jangka to us! There seemed to be no end to the trail of students that found their way to our doorstep, and so we began hosting what we affectionately called Jangka Saturdays, which was a time for students to come to our home for games, crafts, and to practice English.

Crafts especially seemed to hit the spot, as most of these students had never done things I took for granted—stringing beads, cutting from magazines to make collages, and using colored pencils to draw. They'd huddle around our dining room table and choose their color combinations or patterns painstakingly.

Uno was usually a favorite game, and to this day, I have trouble playing it as I got so burnt out after years and years of rounds of this game.

We gathered to love on these kids, give them a sense of family and home, and grow our community of people from Jangka living in the city. We celebrated holidays together, decorating cookies and even reading and acting out the story of Jesus' birth.

Many of these students also studied the Bible with us in one way or another. Danil, who emerged as the leader of this group, procured a Bible all on his own before approaching Ethan to ask him if he'd teach him from it. Danil's younger cousin became my teacher, and we used the Bible as a textbook for me to grow my ability to use spiritual terms in Tibetan.

Some of the Jangka group even joined us for church at various times. Church in China was nothing like what we had experienced growing up. I remember my first Sunday in China when I gathered with other foreign believers for what they called church. We were a small group, somewhere between ten and fifteen people, and we all crowded into someone's living room, with chairs so tightly forming a circle that you would probably be touching someone at some point for a while. At first, it felt hard to sing as someone's eyeballs were very close to my own, staring at me from the other side of the circle. Someone would share from God's word, but often it felt like more of a discussion than a sermon.

I'd soon find out these responsibilities were shared, and I'd better warm up my singing voice and get ready to prepare mini-sermons. We were a team, and that seeped into all areas of life.

An interesting turn in church life happened when our group had dwindled to just seven of us, and we decided to live out how a Tibetan church might gather together to worship God. We chose only to use the Scriptures available to them, which was only a handful of books of the Bible at that point, and pretend that only one of us was literate at a time. We sang songs in Tibetan, danced, and ate our way through Bible discussions because we had all seen up close and personal that Tibetans liked to eat their way through anything. We used drama and skits, and drawings to illustrate God's Word with the hope of making it memorable so that those who could not read would still be able to carry God's Word away with them in their memory and retell it to others.

We learned to appreciate this different kind of church, with only a handful of people crowded around a small coffee table, each person offering something different yet valuable and essential.

We learned to appreciate each other, too. We learned to relax into our skin and not try to be the picture of what we thought we were supposed to be. We were family, really - with different opinions and different ways of doing things and different abilities and strengths. Our natural skills shone through and blessed others in this environment, and our weaknesses were visible and prodded and worked on without embarrassment and with encouragement. We were known and accepted and celebrated.

It was a sweet season that wouldn't last as long as we hoped, as people coming and going in this life were frequent enough that dynamics shifted seemingly overnight. We lost dear ones to understandable things such as schooling difficulties or health or family needs in home countries. But it never made the loss easier. Though a regular part of life, saying goodbye always felt quite miserable and semi-traumatic. When people left, there was a good chance you would never see them again. Often their home country was half a world away from yours, with your meeting place somewhere entirely separate in the great big world. It was a death, in a way. The closeness you experienced that had been forged through trials and challenges faced together in difficult and foreign locations was stripped away at what felt like the drop of a hat.

One day, a family from Jangka was staying at the church host's home, and they got in on the action. As Ethan shared the story about Jesus calming the wind and the waves, he asked us to ponder these questions: What do you like about the story? What didn't you like or didn't you understand? What does this story show us about people? What does this story teach us about Jesus? We had learned these questions as part of a course on storytelling.

At first glance, these questions seem simple. But their straightforwardness made the conversation open easily, made discussion flow, and produced deep thoughts about life and man and his relationship with God. The mother of the family exclaimed that Jesus must not be afraid of anything since He was sleeping through a big storm, and the father said that Jesus must have had to do miracles so that others could see He was not just an ordinary man.

God brought others from Jangka to us as our home soon became a vacation destination for so many of the people we had met when we were up in their neck of the woods. It was so fun to reconnect with people we cared so much about in our own home after they had so warmly welcomed us into theirs. We purchased cots to squeeze into the edges of our apartment that could be ready to go whenever we had a surprise visitor or five surprise visitors!

Once, I got caught two separate times in my PJs by unexpected visitors in a single day. One arrived very early in the morning and the other late in the evening.

One of the most surprising visitors we ever had was my closest friend's boyfriend of over four years. It was surprising because I didn't even know she *had* a boyfriend! I felt almost offended like I wasn't her real friend, but she assured me the reason she was compelled to keep this secret was out of respect. I was older than she was, and she felt it would be rude to talk about boys with me.

Even ShiDa made good on her dreams of visiting the city. I have to hand it to her that she figured out how to get herself down there in a relatively short period of time. She was braver than I thought she'd be, ready to take in the city for the first time. Maybe a little too brave, as I had to grab on to the belt of her robe and pull her back as she took off into eight lanes of traffic without looking right or left or anywhere besides where she wanted to go.

When we showed her the light-up man that signaled when was the appropriate time to walk, she was amazed and couldn't stop talking about it. Her delight in all of the small things while looking in store windows reminded me of a child at an amusement park, and her joy was contagious. I was having so much fun, and so was she.

She was also adventurous in trying my cooking. I prepared a beef roast with potatoes and carrots and bread, hoping that it was similar enough to her diet to be palatable and different enough to feel exotic. She dove in with words of praise and cleaned her plate.

She loved going through my cupboards and having me explain what all of the things were. When she saw my container of spices, she announced that I was a doctor. She didn't ask me if I was; she just declared it. I tried to explain that those little containers were not medicine, and I was not a doctor, but I'm pretty sure I didn't convince her.

She was startled at the sound of an airplane flying overhead and exclaimed how windy it was here in the city. When we explained that it was an airplane, something she had never seen or heard before, she was shocked and delighted. The next time she heard the whooshing sound above her head, she again exclaimed how strong the wind was, and we reminded her that it was an airplane. Oh yes, she said. But she never quite remembered each time a new plane passed by, and we continued to repeat our same conversation.

Our bathroom had a lock on it, which was something entirely foreign for ShiDa and any other visitor from the mountainside. They tended to do their business and *then* lock the door on their way out, closing the door behind them. Our house was a rental, and we had no keys for the door, so we became quite familiar with the neighborhood locksmith and he with our wallet.

When this situation happened with ShiDa as a guest in our home, Ethan joked, "I guess I just don't have a good relationship with bathrooms," which started ShiDa cackling and unable to catch her breath.

We were thankful she could be so lighthearted about the situation. However, we wouldn't expect anything different from her. I silently begged the locksmith to get here soon, as I needed to use my bathroom, which was currently unoccupied and locked.

ShiDa found Ethan's comment hilarious for a specific reason, and she jumped right in to recount one of her favorite stories. While we were staying in her guesthouse, she heard Ethan yelling and yelling "help" one afternoon while she was in her sitting room. She found him locked inside the bathroom at the end of the hall. She couldn't figure out how to get him out of the tiny space with just room for feet on either side of the hole, so she left him there to try and find help in town.

She found a Chinese workman and tried to explain what was happening, but once it became clear that he couldn't understand Tibetan and she couldn't speak Chinese, she took to pulling his arm and dragged him behind her to *show* him the current trouble Ethan had landed himself in.

Ethan was grateful for the assistance, having endured quite an extended time in the bathroom, but this guy couldn't figure a way out, either, and he left to get more tools.

He arrived back with an ax and chopped a chunk of wood off the bottom of the door to loosen whatever had made the door wedge and warp into the current position, and Ethan was freed.

ShiDa found this whole thing immediately gut-busting and couldn't stop teasing Ethan and howling. She seemed completely unfazed by the new aesthetic of a jagged hole in the bottom corner of her bathroom door, nor the privacy it would now take away from her future guests.

Oh yes, Ethan and the bathroom did NOT have a good relationship with each other.

A very short time after ShiDa returned to Jangka, she invited us to celebrate the New Year with her family in their village home. We'd been back in the city in our own home for a few months and felt rested physically, mentally, and emotionally.

ShiDa gave us a private room in their village home, which I didn't even know was possible in Tibetan homes. We had never slept apart from the family in any situation before this one.

ShiDa had also bought a new blanket and even slippers and

placed them by our bed! She must have been taking notes when she visited us in the city. There was an electric blanket on our bed, and I felt like with this bit of privacy and the ability of warmth and the company of ShiDa, I could stay here forever, which turned out to be a good thing because we actually couldn't figure out how to leave.

Whenever we mentioned leaving to ShiDa, she let us know that it wasn't possible and turned and walked away as if the matter had already been concluded. She said the days were not auspicious, and no driver was willing to drive on the road. With ShiDa, it was hard to tell if she was telling the truth or instead enforcing her way of having us stay for her pleasure, but either way, there wasn't much we could do. We were enjoying our time, and if she was willing to wrangle us into feeling stuck on purpose, we must not be overstaying our welcome. We made ourselves at home.

Our brief visit to her home lasted for over a week.

We drank pounds of butter and were included in all of the traditional elements of the holiday. I made holiday "cookies" with ShiDa's daughter-in-law, dropping sugarless strips of dough into hot, bubbling oil, and I fried duck over the big wood-burning stove.

ShiDa's daughter-in-law moved into the family house when she married ShiDa's oldest son, which was the way of doing things here. She was affectionately known as the "Namah," the Tibetan word for a daughter-in-law that does all the work.

A daughter-in-law does a lot of the heavy lifting for the new family. Besides cooking and cleaning inside the house for the family members, she often spends her days with the livestock or in the fields, coming home to wash clothes by hand and get supper on the table.

It looked like a tough life to me, but the Namah seemed happy. I know there's always more to the story, but her smile looked genuine. She joined in the playful banter of life, and she seemed just as much a part of life and family as everyone else. She married at age eighteen, an arranged marriage, and had been at this life for twelve years already, producing two children along the way, which was also essential for a Namah to accomplish.

At her arrival into the family, ShiDa's husband gifted her with clothing and kitchen stuff - pots and pans and ladles, the customary bride price. She told me she stumbled unprepared into the role of Namah, not even knowing how to cook, but she learned quickly by trial and error.

We visited all of ShiDa's living relatives, passing out small gifts, such as fake packs of gum that shock you as you try to pull out a piece. We visited all of her dead relatives, too, watching ShiDa's family burn food for them, hoping their bellies would be filled as they wandered the spirit world as ghosts.

We picnicked with other villagers in the middle of a freezing cold and blustery and windy afternoon. They said no matter the weather; no one misses this traditional yearly village picnic. ShiDa's husband was unusually chatty and recollected the first time he ever saw a car and a Chinese person at age fifteen. His parents had lived through and survived the Great Famine, and I felt like there was living history in front of me as he shared more of his story and theirs.

On New Year's Day, with the tables laden with food and colors and decorations, ShiDa asked if Ethan would pray, as she had seen us do that many times before.

It was such a special moment, surrounded by generations of family on a super special day, with plenty abounding both on the table in front of us and our hearts. We were feeling strong, joyful, and connected. My stress levels reached earlier in the summer had melted away, and my insecurities about speaking Tibetan in front of Ethan were a distant memory. This trip felt easy and fun, and meaningful. He thanked God for all of His blessings, this family, and His place in the world and our lives.

As Ethan's words rang out in Tibetan, it was strange to think that probably the God-above-all-gods' name had never been addressed aloud in this way in the history of the world in this particular village.

That moment felt powerful and sacred.

When we finally procured a ride out of the village, we had a very tight schedule! We had received many invitations from friends, and we wanted to make good on our word to stop in. We weren't confident enough yet to follow in the steps of ShiDa and say, "Oh, yes, I'm coming," while never actually planning to arrive. And so we bumped and jostled around to fifteen different homes to wish everyone a Happy New Year.

During this time, we received an interesting proposal. A Tibetan family was going down to the city from Jangka, and they were wondering if we would want to do a house swap with them. Their daughter worked in the city and couldn't get time off to come home for the New Year celebrations, so they wanted to go to her.

They didn't want to stay in a guesthouse, as it would make it hard for them to celebrate in a familiar and fun way to them. They wanted a place to cook and gather and be a family.

We said yes. We found it especially funny that while they'd be trying to figure out what a coffee pot was, we'd be falling asleep under strips of drying meat.

It was so fun to play house out in Jangka. It was a small apartment above a shop on the main drag in town. Carrying keys to my home, I'd climb the stairs and open the outside door from a balcony that ran along the way to a handful of other connected apartments. The door opened to a small, cement kitchen with everything you needed and nothing you didn't need. There was a bathroom attached, with a flushable squat toilet and shower head, although warm water was not possible out in these parts yet, so I'm not sure who would be brave enough to use the showerhead to shower. Also, of course, the running water was very sporadic, and so much of the kitchen was taken up with large barrels that we would fill with water when the water was accessible to use for the majority of the time when there was no water. I did enjoy the novelty of being able to heat water for a sponge bath whenever it struck my fancy.

There was a living room with only a small pathway to walk between the furniture and the coffee table and two tiny bedrooms with enough room for a bed and a small armoire. Yes, everything was tiny. Very small. But adequate. Very adequate.

I cooked on the two-burner stove, and we even invited friends to OUR home for meals and tea and to watch the Olympics.

Yes, they also had a TV, and when the electricity was on, we were able to watch some of the actual Olympics. It was strange to feel connected to the bigger world when we were hunkered down in this place that usually feels so cut off from everything else.

Our days were full, but our evenings were restful, a combination that felt right.

When we boarded the bus to go home, I felt alive. Happy. Motivated and strong. We were seated next to a random stranger who repeated over and over in English, "My shoes don't fit my feet." It was the one phrase someone had taught him in English along the way, and he was determined to get his use out of it as he had found an English-speaking person.

A Tibetan village

CHAPTER 29

*W*e stood outside the busy hospital on the busy street in the busy city and wondered what the people were like that were supposed to meet us. Some relatives of Teacher Sunshine from Jangka had come down to the city to get help for a sick child, and Teacher Sunshine had arranged for us to go to them as they tried to find their footing in a foreign city. They did not know a single person in this massive metropolis, and I found it ironic and lovely that we were the closest thing to family they could find as foreigners ourselves.

Chinese culture and language couldn't be any more different from Tibetan culture and language, and city life and expectations were a far cry from anything this couple carried with them from their tiny village a world away. To make it from there to here could only mean that their child was very sick. Very, very sick.

A man began waving to us from a distance. We were easy to spot as the only non-Asians in this sea of people. It never hurt that Ethan's head generally stuck out far above all of the other heads. As the man approached, I knew he looked familiar but couldn't quite place him. My mind rumbled through its files and finally landed.

The painter!

It was the man who had been precariously hanging from Teacher Sunshine's windowsill and had come down and chatted with Teacher Sunshine's dad and me in the grass.

I hadn't seen him since.

Until now.

Remember how I warned you that I wished I could have warned him?

Well.

Here we were.

He led us to the bedside of his one-and-a-half-year-old daughter. I'm not sure what I expected to see. In some ways, she seemed like a one-and-a-half-year-old girl lying on a bed.

But something wasn't right. She laid utterly still, and I couldn't tell if her eyes were able to focus, or actually if they could see anything at all, even though they were wide open. Almost too open and not blinking the way they maybe should have been.

She looked so little lying there, her diaper exposed under a hospital gown on the adult-sized bed. Her fingers and toes seemed too small to be sick, at least this ill, as she was supposed to be playing or crying or making toddler demands or noise or something or anything.

She was one of many toddlers stretched out in a line of beds surrounded by other parents willing their children to recover.

The doctor was hesitant to provide hope, even as they poured medicine into her IV daily. The little girl remained a shell of the little girl she was just days before.

Running, laughing, the darling of the family home.

She had taken a fall and received a small puncture wound in her mouth from chopsticks, which didn't seem to be a big deal at all.

But then she got sick.

They brought her to the village doctor, who told them she had a cold and would be fine. But her fever grew worse and worse until she became unresponsive.

They rushed down the mountainside as fast as the mountainsides allow and arrived at the hospital after over twelve hours of travel.

The doctor explained that the puncture in her mouth had introduced bacteria into her bloodstream. An infection had set in, and the infection had reached the brain with treatment delayed.

Their baby girl had stopped eating and talking. She was unable to sit up or even hold her head up. No one was sure if she could even see.

It felt unbelievable. How could this happen? How can moments and instants change years and decades? Lifetimes?

If only time could be rewound. If only things had happened just a little bit differently. If only they had arrived at the hospital for help a little bit earlier.

But it can't, and it didn't, and what is, is, no matter that it just doesn't seem possible.

Hope rested on a cocktail of medicines, and we all willed something to work. It was hard for me to read the doctor, but he did not look hopeful to my untrained eyes. He continued to say the girl would be in the hospital for a long time but never expounded on what a long time might mean.

We visited the hospital regularly and wished that our presence could bring them just a minute of something different than sad, and if not that, then at least a knowledge that they were not completely and utterly alone. I didn't see too much emotion from the painter, who had grown into an actual person with a name, or his wife. And maybe that's what I should have noticed. The emotion was absent, which is a telltale sign that grief and sadness are present. Perhaps more than present. Maybe all-consuming. Tibetans seem to always smile.

But there were no smiles now.

We brought them a Chinese checkers game and a newly released book in Tibetan, *The Lion, the Witch, and the Wardrobe* by CS Lewis, even though we weren't sure if they could read. It had beautifully drawn Tibetan-style pictures, which was something, and we thought, as a painter himself, he might appreciate the art.

We brought instant packets of butter tea (yes, that was a thing! Just add hot water!) and snacks, willing these objects to bring just an ounce of comfort to these miserable days. They probably didn't, but I needed them to know I saw them and that they were loved and not forgotten.

I considered that I might be a burden, sucking energy that they didn't have just by making my presence known and forcing them to lift their heads and say hello. Still, it seemed like we were giving them just a little bit of life, and I decided it was essential to keep riding my bicycle to the hospital to drop in as often as I could.

The room itself had a very, very forlorn and desperate feeling. A single chair was shoved too close to each bed to give a nursing parent a place to sit. There was no room for these families to move around, and the despair hung like a cloud above them all. The sadness made the room feel even smaller. There was no TV or pictures on the wall. There was one squat toilet behind a door at the end of the room. The cement walls were cracked and dirty, and it reminded everyone that they'd rather be anywhere than here. Here, where the news was bad, and the hope was quickly seeping out through those cracks in the wall.

Teacher Sunshine's dad had now arrived, and I finally understood that the painter was family, not just a workman, which puts my experiences into a tighter package. As the family patriarch, Teacher Sunshine's dad was paying the mounting bills and watching over the situation. His Chinese was also better than the others', having served the police force, and he was a decent intermediary between the doctors and the parents, relieving me of some of my shaky-at-best duties.

The days stretched into weeks, and after a month, we received the phone call that they were being released from the hospital. It was the first glimmer of joy I saw in either of them. Or maybe relief is a better word for what I saw. They were going to bring their baby home.

Outwardly, there had been little sign of improvement, but the doctor told them just to keep giving her medicine, and slowly, slowly, she could get better. I wondered if the doctor had actually said those words - that she COULD get better. Or if they had just wanted to hear those words so badly that they had.

They were told to return with the baby in one month.

When they returned for the check-up, they returned to us. We prepared their beds and a hot meal for them after their long journey. We were happy to see that the painter's daughter seemed to have grown and put on a bit of weight in the month they were at home. However, she was still unable to sit up, walk or talk.

When the doctors reported at their follow-up visit that she was indeed recovering slowly and that, over time, she would continue to get better and that they did not need to come back for any more check-ups in the future, I was worried. No more check-ups? That did not sound like they were expecting progress. But in those situations, you need to hang on to any kernel of possible good news, so I grabbed on alongside the painter and his wife and looked forward to the day their daughter was back to her bubbly little self.

It wasn't long before they traveled to the city again, even though they had been told there was no need. In fact, the painter and his wife and daughter came back and forth and back and forth, round and round again, in search of help. The help they had been told was not available, but the help they couldn't help begging and pleading and searching for. I mean, what else could they do? And so we looked, tried, and hoped, but nothing seemed to change the situation.

With each visit, we met more family members. During one visit, the toddler's other set of grandparents accompanied the painter's family, and they settled into life with us with lots of chatting and questions and exploring our home. The grandmother was fascinated by my bread machine. As she watched me put in all ingredients, I explained how the machine worked. As I closed the lid, she said, "There's a spoon in there!" I said, "yes," thinking she was referring to the little paddle that kneads the bread. Only when I took out the finished bread did I see the metal spoon stuck straight through the loaf!

The grandfather was enamored with the maps we kept in our home, and Ethan tried to teach him how to read one. He was also full of spiritual questions, and we had lots of time to answer them all, which only led to more questions. It was a fulfilling talk for all of us. Even though the circumstances that had caused us to meet more and more of this extended family were heartbreaking, we were so thankful for these precious people who became so familiar to us. Our lives had become so entrenched with theirs that it was hard to remember not knowing them at some point.

My life *still* feels so entwined with theirs, and I think there are a couple of reasons for that. During this season of life, one day, while I was drinking my morning cup of coffee, my stomach did a little lurchy thing. It was a sensation I hadn't felt before. It felt a bit like being car sick, but I was perfectly still, sitting in a chair. It was an unpleasant sensation and surprisingly strong, even though I would come to know that this was a mild mani-festation of this particular sickness.

I was pregnant.

Watching the painter's daughter's situation unfold and evolve felt so different now, as I could feel my own little one swimming in my belly. I felt their pain, worry, and desperation freshly, acutely, and powerfully. The situation was more real than ever. How do you walk through grief like that? My despair for them deepened, while the excitement for our growing family tagged right along too. A little life was growing inside of me, waiting to come out and call me mama.

I had a few days to revel in this secret before full-blown morning sickness consumed every minute of every day and night. The first few months passed in a fog as I just tried to survive while simultaneously wishing my days away. Morning sickness seemed to be one of those things that you just can't understand until you experience it. I certainly didn't.

We found a reputable doctor not far from where we lived at what was called the Women's and Children's Hospital. It was always more than bustling with hordes of women with big bellies trying to push past each other to get to their next assigned location. This was complicated because half of us were carrying open cups of urine up and down the stairwells and through the jostling crowds, trying to make our way to the front of the line to get our blood drawn. I like to think we were all a bit more gentle than the grocery store jockeying for position in "lines," but I can't say I noticed a huge difference.

Appointments were stressful but exciting. After paying four dollars for both our doctor's visit and our ultrasound, we were amazed that the beautiful blob on the screen would be ours. The doctor whispered the sex of our baby to us, even though the sign above my head clearly said that was illegal. Because of the one-child policy in China, they did not want people selectively aborting babies of a sex they did not wish for their only child.

I'd always wanted to be a mom, and somewhere deep down inside, I always knew I would be. I couldn't imagine my life turning out any other way. I was good with kids, loved to hold babies, and being the oldest of five kids myself, it felt like I knew a thing or two about it all.

The thought of needing to slow down a bit and spend more time at home was appealing. I wasn't worried about exchanging the hectic and lively life I had for a more simple one. I was ready to snuggle, nurture, and feed my little bundle of joy. Besides, we would be one of those families that just went with the flow and brought our baby along for the ride. Easy peasy.

The thought of raising my child in a foreign country was also appealing to me and didn't make me nervous in the least. I thought about what a great perspective we could give our child as just part of their ordinary life. I felt like it was a marvelous gift we were going to be able to offer our child. They would grow up speaking at least two or three languages fluently and dance in and out of various cultures with ease. They would grow up instinctively knowing the value of all people, not being scared of differences, and benefit significantly from being exposed to so many divergent ways of doing things.

Being pregnant in this place also made me feel more connected to those around me. There was no chance to pretend I was playing house in this metropolis, as I was laying down roots and starting a family. I felt like one of them in a more profound way than I ever had before.

I somehow managed to keep up with my studies in between throwing up and hosting guests, and all along, a little baby grew bigger and bigger in my womb, waiting to experience this place in not too long for themself.

CHAPTER 30

I was feverishly packing a bag for Thailand. At our routine visit to the doctor, he expressed concern that our baby would come early. We had planned to cross the border to give birth in a place with better medical care, and it seemed like our exit date had just been pushed up by a couple of weeks.

I shouldn't have been surprised that things turned out differently than planned. My pregnancy had seemed fraught with minor complications: low amniotic fluid, abnormalities in organs suspected on ultrasounds, spotting, and bed rest.

There were frantic internet searches, as I'm sure take place in every pregnancy. I worried. I cried. I was reassured that most of the time, these things mean nothing. I was reassured that the baby and I were healthy. Fine.

Probably.

And so it seemed that we were both healthy and fine as our little girl made her tiny way into that delivery room in Thailand in the middle of the night, two weeks early.

We were given a private room, something they had told me was not a guarantee, as there was only one, and it was first come, first serve. There were no options for pain relief, and I think what worried my first-time-birther brain the most was the possibility of needing to be close enough to touch another mother trying to give birth and listening to her screams next to mine.

But as luck, or grace, would have it, I had my own room. The nurses only entered once an hour to put a stethoscope on my belly to listen to the baby's heartbeat. They would chatter about what they heard to me in the Thai language, one in which I only knew a handful of greetings, the numbers, and a few staple dishes, but somehow the language barrier didn't seem to affect a single thing. When the doctor arrived, she came in to greet me and, in perfect English, with only a slight accent, said, when you feel like you want to push out the baby, just touch that red button on the wall.

And away she went.

The pain was terrible; no need to try and describe it because there are no words to describe that kind of pain. When I felt like my body would be ripped in two, I pushed the red button. Not because I thought I was ready to push, but because I was ready to die.

The world changes when you have a child. I was prepared to roll her into our life the same way Ethan had rolled into my life. Smoothly, without bumps or waves or whiplash.

I was not prepared.

The only thing harder to describe than the pain of labor is

the love that fills your heart with the birth of a child. That love took all of the limelight, and our new show began.

It should be simple. The only thing I needed to do as a mom was to care for and protect my child physically and give her what she needed emotionally.

But I was not prepared for how much work that took.

Everything in life took a backseat because, of course, it did.

I was not prepared to feel fear while changing my child's diaper because she felt so fragile or when all five pounds thirteen ounces of her seemed too slippery to bathe. I was not prepared for the effort required at all twelve feedings throughout the night and day. I was not prepared to help my child sleep. I thought that was something babies just did.

Most of the time, I didn't have time to look up from whatever immediate need I was focused on before scrambling on to the next.

As the love for this child consumed me, I was distraught that it seemed like my baby was struggling. She seemed unable to be comforted or consoled. I would have given anything for that poor, sweet thing not to experience pain or sadness or anything other than only goodness both now and forever, and I was willing to give my absolute everything to try and make that happen for her.

And I did try—absolutely everything. Somehow, we just couldn't get there. We took her to the doctor but were told that babies cry, and not all babies sleep a lot. We tried medicine for reflux. I changed my diet. Nothing helped. We limped and shuffled through those days with brains on overdrive and bodies screaming for sleep and, if not sleep, any second of relief.

I was not prepared for how much her wails and cries would be so intertwined with my insides that knowing where her pain began and mine started wasn't something I could ever quite figure out. I grew more and more unsettled and then eventually unequivocally tormented.

Those first months with our dear, sweet, longed-for child were the most challenging days of my life. I would do them all again, and in between the screams and the feeding struggle and the endless nights when none of us slept, we marveled at this amazing and beautiful little girl whom we couldn't believe we got to call our own. She was perfect and beautiful and everything we could have ever asked for, but we just couldn't soothe her even after reading every book and trying every tip.

At five months old, I had given everything I had in me to this little one. There was nothing left for me to give, but still, she needed more. She was having a hard time figuring out how to exist in this new world, but what I had to offer wasn't enough, so now what? Everything babies were supposed to do just didn't happen for us. She didn't smile. She didn't laugh. She didn't eat. She didn't sleep.

I never once thought that there might be something deeper going on. That there may be an underlying reason for all of the issues we faced. I assumed it was my failure. My incompetency. I had planned to be so good at this mothering job. I worked harder than I ever had before at anything to help my daughter survive and grow and be content. But it wasn't enough.

I tried every feeding method a million times and then a million more, and still, she gagged and sputtered and struggled. The world felt like too much for her, and I sunk down there right with her. The world was starting to feel like too much for me, too. And then the bottom of the world and everything fell out.

She got sick. And she didn't get better. Our emergency evacuation insurance that we were sure we would never have to use flew us out of China and to the United States. She got better from that acute illness, but almost as soon as we were back in China, she got sick again. And then the issues came rolling in, one after another, faster than we could handle.

Living with a child in China was different from living without a child in China.

My first taste of life in China with a baby was in the bathroom at the airport after just arriving from Thailand when she was just a nugget of a thing. I was trying to change her diaper, but I couldn't even see what I was doing because all the Chinese grandmas were getting their heads and hands in for a closer look or touch. At the same time, a group of teenagers all whipped out their cell phones and began snapping pictures.

We heard the words "so cute!" countless times a day and "she's not dressed warm enough" about the same number of times. On stroller walks, or should I say stroller pauses, we were stopped many times for people to snag a look. She was like a mini-celebrity. Everyone loved her.

Telling me what I was doing wrong was also a common

thread of conversations. For a person who was more insecure about motherhood than she had ever been about anything in her entire life, it was a point of major contention and anxiety for me. I know culturally it was their way of showing they cared, and they did this to their own as well, but most of the time it was much more than I could bear.

We slowly emerged back into life as our daughter grew, but things took on a different flavor than before. I wasn't the mom who continued with life as it had always been, plugging my kid into the previous way's rhythms. I was home. I went from spending most of my time outside of my home to most of my time inside my home.

This reckoning was very difficult for me, even though I was sure I had been ready for the transition. I viewed myself as a high-powered worker transformed into an old lady who rarely left the house and cried a lot overnight. It was harder to pinpoint what I had to offer this country and people when I spent all of my time making our own little family's life happen.

But here's what I eventually figured out.

Cross-cultural fields need families. We might be slower and get less done and not tackle the seemingly hardest jobs on the list at times, but we certainly can provide much-needed things that aren't as easy for other categories of people.

There is comfort and security and often a hot meal in the homes of families. How often did we open our home to singles or short-term passersby on Christmas or other holidays when the lack of family could almost break one's spirit? Twinkling lights and pumpkin pie and a baby to cuddle that is yours for the day can fill in those losses, not perfectly, but enough.

When nieces and nephews are too far away to touch, the children of other families are there to close the gap, and they, of course, need honorary Aunts and Uncles as well.

Besides, most of the Jangka students we had gotten to know over the years were moving along right next to us and leaving university, getting jobs, getting married, and having babies. We were all moving into adulthood, and with it came responsibilities and cares, and big decisions.

One relationship of mine specifically felt like it came full circle. A village girl had worked hard at school in her hometown. She had made it into a boarding school a few hours from her parents and was then selected to attend university in the city where I first met her. She was learning about Chinese city life at the same time as I was, both foreigners in very different ways. We were officially university students together, and our paths crossed many times. There were certain years when I was her teacher and other years when she was my teacher. I had stayed in her village home, and she had slept in my city home. We had talked about all things lodged deep in our hearts, and we had laughed about silly things. We had made it through the earth-quake together and had sorted through the emotions that came with that side-by-side. We had shared many meals and walked many miles together. She had gotten a job and then married at the same time as me, and our babies had been born within months of each other. We were existing through all parts of life together. The good, the bad, the ugly, the beautiful, the hard, the easy, and every little moment in between. We were moving through life's milestones together. Walking through these life stages together in this country definitely made me feel like I was no longer an outsider looking in. I'm not sure I was nor would ever be an insider looking out, but I definitely felt wedged into this life in a way that felt quite permanent.

This land was where I had found my husband and was the place where I was raising my first child, and I don't know of any more robust indicator of the level of integration my heart felt with my surroundings. It was a conscious choice to live fully there, and I never had thoughts of one day returning to America. I had accepted this country as my own, and I expected the years to unfurl before us in this place we called home.

CHAPTER 31

Some of the first biographies I read were about translation work in the jungles among people without written languages. It just seemed so exotic and beautiful and consequential. I can still see old photos in my mind of a white lady sitting with a tribal woman with little clothing and a big piece of equipment and all her notes and pens that I saw in a book when I was young. To me, translation work was the pinnacle of it all.

Just after our daughter turned 1, Ethan asked me if I would be willing to help with a translation project. I couldn't say yes fast enough. We were also going to do a switcheroo, something I realize is a perk of this lifestyle that not many people in regular life can do. It meant I got to leave the house every day while Ethan stayed home and experienced a day in the life of a stay-at-home parent. Oh, how I wanted him to experience my heavy workload and grow in appreciation of me, and oh, how I wanted to escape into the freedom of going to the bathroom whenever I wanted and sipping a hot beverage that was hot, all the while basking in silence.

I'm going to be honest here. It was every bit as great as I'd imagined and hoped. I didn't struggle to leave my baby behind, and I skipped out that door and took a huge gulp of the polluted air; for a moment, it felt like everything was going to be okay. I felt alive.

I should have let this moment teach me more about myself because, looking back, it feels so obvious. As much as I was determined to be a stay-at-home mom and let motherhood be my primary identity for this next season of life, I shouldn't have allowed it to be my only thing, even when I couldn't figure out how there would ever be time for anything other.

I was an extrovert, a worker, a dreamer, and cutting those things off me was doing no good, least of all to myself or anyone else near me, namely Ethan and my daughter. I needed something "other" to keep me going, even if it added one more thing to the pot. And I should have learned to ask for help much sooner than I did.

It took a long time for me to realize that giving to the outside world, even if stressful for a handful of moments, actually gave me energy and fulfilled me in a more-than-necessary way for my mental health. Even if done out of a place of depletion, work was life-giving for me. It wasn't a simple 1+1=2 equation, but it was a fact. It was finding the balance that was the hard part.

For me, sharing the load of day-to-day parenting, even for just a short while, helped me feel not so desperately alone and perpetually lonely. Furthermore, working on the translation project made me feel like I was a contributor to something outside of me.

Sitting at that table, just me and those words and my computer on that day, was a moment to remember for a lifetime. I thought of those pictures I had seen as a young girl. And now, here I was, decades later, sitting on a very similar chair at a very similar table. Well, it was a fluorescent-colored chair at a local fast food joint that served an interesting fusion of KFC-like foods with traditional Chinese dishes. Scratch the mashed potatoes, and add the rice. There were skyscrapers surrounding me, viewable from the second-floor deck where I sat, with the sounds and pollution of city buses and bicycle horns filling the air. Anyway, I digress.

Back to this perfect moment in my life, even if it was slightly un-jungle-like.

Fulfillment. That is what this moment was. I had climbed my mountain, and here I stood, claiming this summit as my own. The noise of struggle faded away, and I was immersed in this job, in this labor of love and passion. That moment was the start of a whole lot of hard work, but I was ready. The work felt like it had been waiting for me.

I remembered back to the early days of language learning when I learned that the Tibetan word for the airplane was iron chicken and a typical greeting was not something that loosely translated as "how are you" but instead "have you eaten yet"? Turtles were bony frogs, and gloves were called hand covers. Learning the language of these people was about way more than just words, but about learning how they saw the world.

Sometimes we wondered if we spent too long with our noses in books while other co-workers went on to do exciting-sounding things like starting businesses or teaching full-time. But I don't regret it. Language gave us the possibility of knowing people and the ability to exchange information and share Jesus profoundly and thoroughly. It did take a long time. We studied for a decade, and still, we could have kept on.

I read the foreign script and diligently recorded the translated words on my computer, knowing that these very words held power that could change lives. And I reveled in the fact that I got to live this moment—this monumental moment inside a slightly grimy restaurant next to a giant poster of a cartoon chicken.

While my life was flying high outside of my doors, our life at home was hard. I moved through my days on overdrive. I'd rise early and make three batches of soy milk for my daughter, whose stomach couldn't seem to tolerate absolutely anything. I'd wash clothes every day, hanging each item up piece by piece outside my window to dry. I'd prepare whatever I was in charge of for our weekly church service. I'd cook meals and clean. Often guests would show up in the afternoon, and I tried to give them the love and attention I wanted to provide them with so badly and that they deserved. All while I was tending and caring for my baby girl with relentless needs.

I remember the first time someone talked about my daughter in a way that assumed she was different. Right before she turned one, the woman spoke so matter-of-factly for just a moment about the difficulties she assumed my daughter would face, as if I somehow had access to this information. I tucked that comment out of reach and carried on, confused.

Slowly, others made comments. The doctor we saw gently

asked me questions that felt out of place, like if my baby felt like she might slip right through my hands when I held her up. I shook my head no, but it came out more like a question than a solid answer when I said no verbally. The doctor said, "Does she feel a little wobbly, like Jello?" Now I was sure I had answered correctly. I had never thought of my baby like Jello.

But then, she still sent us on a wild goose chase to find therapists and equipment to encourage our daughter to move and babble and eat and play. I knew milestones were passing us by, but all kids develop at their own pace, right?

We searched far and wide to consult medical professionals from China and others we managed to rustle up from France, the United States, Australia, Singapore, and even Korea. They all pointed out more and more concerns and had varied approaches to how they thought we should deal with what they saw.

The issues were endless and only got more pronounced and severe. Medically we continued to battle sicknesses of all sorts. More than that, her little body didn't naturally do the things everyone else's bodies did, and we had to both trick her into drinking milk and then start the long process of helping the leftovers make their way out the other end. Forget any kind of eating. She'd gag at the sight of anything resembling food.

Developmentally she hadn't moved on from sitting, and we were nearing the eighteen-month mark. She didn't smile or make many sounds.

We could easily recognize when she was happy, as even if the way she reacted to different situations wasn't what you'd typically expect, we could read her like any parent can read their child.

She was happy if she started moving her tongue in and out of her mouth. She loved soft sounds repeated over and over, like the click of a wooden spoon. She loved books more than any toy and would sit contentedly on the lap of anyone willing to read to her for as long as they would read. She loved to be outside, and from very early on, she would follow animals with her eyes, much more than she would track people's movements. We dubbed our countless stroller walks throughout the day the puppy patrol, and I knew she could be content if we found a canine out for a walk. Lucky for us, there are always dogs out for walks in China.

We loved our life with our child and reveled in how she discovered her world and connected with us.

She brought us as much joy as any child has ever brought any parent, but it didn't mean life was easy. And while I had no problem finding God's hand in giving me this beautiful daughter to call my own, I had a hard time seeing God's hand in this life of therapy and doctors that now took up most of my waking moments. It seemed that just to perform the daily duties required to keep my daughter alive, I lost the ability to do anything else. I wondered what benefit there was to even being here in China. I could do the same in America, but have family around and do it in English and with snacks I liked.

I was never angry at God. I always believed that He was in control and had a plan. I never questioned His ways in a way that felt like He was getting it wrong. I never doubted His goodness.

But I wondered what His purpose could be in all of this. For the life of me, I could not figure out how this could work out for the good of our overseas work in general.

While the whole big world needed saving, I was locked in my tiny apartment helping my daughter build muscle strength on an exercise ball and brushing her gums with strange nubby brushes they said would desensitize her mouth enough to try to get some calories down and in.

And then, one day, I learned that sometimes existing is enough on its own to make a difference.

When a friend's grandfather was in the hospital, preparing for heart surgery, my baby girl and I ventured out to show that we cared because I did care, and showing up was the only thing I thought I might have the strength or time to do.

We made our way through the busy hospital to find this man alone, less than an hour from the start of his surgery. Not all that long ago, I had sat in his family's living room, located eight hours down a very curvy and dusty road from the room where we now sat. We had watched a basketball game on the small screen while we chatted about the weather and picked nuts and dried fruit out of a bowl on the small wooden table between us. This baby girl that I now carried on my hip had then been curled up on my insides, growing big enough and strong enough to come out into the world when the time was right. Ethan had gone up the mountains further than I had, to sleep in a tent for a week and teach at an English camp where no foreigner had ever stepped foot before. The altitude there was too high for the little one growing in my womb to adjust to, so I had stayed down here with friends, where it was safe.

It had been a weird feeling, being left behind, and part of me had wondered if it was a taste of what it could feel like in just a few short months. If it was, I wondered if I might not like it just as much as I thought I was going to. I didn't want to miss out on anything, and an English camp for kids in a Tibetan village was my cup of tea.

But here I was, with my daughter dressed in a cute dress and a bright headband on her head, meeting with this grandfather again in a more significant situation.

As soon as our greetings were exchanged in his hospital room, he reached for my girl, and I watched in surprise as she sat so contently in his arms as he reclined under the covers of his bed. I saw how her little body calmed his soul and marveled at him, smiling tenderly at her new, fresh, little life, just as his old life was fighting to beat on for just a little bit longer.

At that moment, that 86-year-old man needed my daughter.

Her value to that man was blatantly obvious; there was no way I or anyone else could deny it. She played a role in calming his mind and heart that no one else played at that moment. While I stood next to his bed, letting my presence be a statement that he was not forgotten, my daughter's warm body pressed into his arms and provided the human touch he would not have received without her in a moment that was hard and lonely and scary.

My daughter's life had value. She mattered and was significant and had work to do here on this planet. That man's life was made better just because she existed precisely as she was, nothing more, nothing less.

That day, even though I had learned how to, at times, put on whatever face was needed for the current situation, I, too, had no strength to pretend I was anything other than what I was. I was just me, standing in a hospital room, ragged, probably disheveled, and barely keeping my eyes open.

But showing up helped. It meant something. It had an impact. It made a difference. It actually made a difference.

It was hard for me to know what impact our years in China had on those we met briefly and on those we got close to, but the glimpses that I could most clearly catch on to were the moments like these.

When I slowed down. When I paused.

When I wasn't trying, but when I looked at someone and stayed.

We all just want to be remembered and cared about just as we are in whatever stage or moment, or situation of life we find ourselves in.

It's what I wanted.

One day, toward the end of a particularly low time of my hidden and unknown depression, a woman I didn't know too well peered at me a little bit too long and a little bit too hard and leaned in and said, "You're the only mother she has. Good or bad, you're it. So get rid of any thoughts of inadequacy."

Her words were not extremely gracious. She said a few other things that felt jarring. She also said a few other things that I knew were meant to be loving, even if I didn't know how to receive them in that way. But she tried. She saw me. She decided not to let me sit alone but scooted her way in and did her best to show me I was not alone and that I was remembered, and she cared enough to put herself into an uncomfortable situation to try and help me, even if she didn't get it quite right.

And that was all I needed, even though that was all I didn't want. That tiny minute of someone pushing into my business and my misery, whether wanted or not, changed things for me. Her words were enough to make me rise and put on my boxing gloves and fight.

Being seen matters.

Jesus walked among the people, looked at their hurts, and didn't turn away. He stopped and talked to the woman caught in adultery even while everyone else wanted to stone her to death. But seeing her, really looking at her, He saved her life. Letting the hemorrhaging woman in and close brought healing to her body and soul. He went to the man with legions of demons when everyone else had pushed him into the wilderness, out of sight and out of mind.

He called out lack of faith when He saw it but then took those with little faith by the hand and said, "I've got you even when you don't have it in yourself to believe."

On the flip side, letting others look at me and stay even at my worst also produced some interesting revelations about what outward impact our lives can have in the most unexpected ways.

A few months into being first-time parents, I was convinced our marriage was crumbling. After having lived every moment together and loving every moment together, we had become complete ships passing in the night. There was no conversation other than communicating about what needs needed to be met and how to get it done. We had become a team, but every other part of our seemingly perfect relationship had up and disappeared.

But one day, a Jangka student looked up at me and said, "Your husband's good to you, isn't he?"

I answered honestly, "Yes, he is."

And then she said, "And you respect him, don't you?"

Again, I answered honestly and said, "Yes, I do."

I would never have been able to put those things about our marriage in words as succinctly as this young girl with long hair that had never been cut and a shy smile between her acne-covered cheeks did. Still, both of those statements were entirely true and highly accurate. I knew then that God could use who we were in Him, and even our marriage in its most challenging days, to bring life and hope to others, even in our darkest days. Existing could still be enough.

The mess was there. There was no strength to cover up any of our messes that first year as new parents. We were on full display for any to see what lay underneath all of the pretty polish that usually went on the outside.

But it was here that it seemed people connected the most. Maybe it was because the mess felt more real and solid than anything else they had seen. They didn't have to dig through all the extras to see the bones and the heart underneath it all.

At my worst, I learned that impact meant being you, owning it, and letting others see it. It meant no pretending, not waiting until you had it all together, but just being as complicated and confused and muddled as you are at any given moment, while keeping your eyes on Jesus.

Because that's all we have to offer anyway, right?

A finger and a life pointing to the one we cling to. A voice that says, "I know there is hope, even if I don't always feel it or live like it, and even when I need someone else to remind me that it's there."

I've noticed that living vulnerably and honestly has made me a soft landing spot for others. When people see the chaos and clutter I'm working with, they're more comfortable showing me that they have their own internal jumbles. Everyone breathes a little easier. The broken and cracked and unsure woman I am makes me authentic and trustworthy to others and seems to be where others are okay to settle into.

It has brought a newfound sense of freedom in not needing to paint a picture I think others want to see but being comfortable with who I am and where I'm at in my journey. I was forced into living this way when anxiety and depression and a child with special needs arrived on top of an already stressful life. Still, I will boldly proclaim that it is an acquirement I'd probably go ahead and purchase again, even if it cost me the same as it had the first go-round.

We've all got stuff. That's for sure. And the energy it takes to hide it, shush it, and cover it up is not worth the energy expended.

We all want to be worthy of love, and we often think the only way to be worthy is to make ourselves better enough, good enough. But that is the entire heart of the gospel, right? We can never be good enough, and that's why we need Jesus. And Jesus' message is clear.

While we were yet sinners, He died for us. What greater love is there than this, that a man lay down his life for another?

We are already loved. Now we just get to be.

So the best way I can figure to impact others for the glory of the almighty God is by living snuggled up next to each other through anything and everything and continuing to look at Jesus, and putting one foot in front of the other clumsily alongside those that happen to be right there next to me, speaking to them of the reason for the hope that is in me.

How did I point to a God of love in a way that was itself actually loving?

By letting others into my physical space, my world, my biggest hurts, and biggest joys, and my everyday ploddings while I clung desperately to Jesus even while I fumbled and bumbled and tumbled my way through life. Saying out loud to both myself and the person next to me, Jesus is enough for me. And He loves me - just as I am.

And He loves you too - just as you are.

Cast your cares upon Him and rest. Fully known and fully loved by the God-above-all-gods.

Teaching English

CHAPTER 32

*W*e couldn't get our daughter to eat. And I don't mean during a particular stretch of time. I mean ever. She was not walking, not talking, and most concernedly, not eating.

I was pregnant with our second child, and we were due to return to the states for our every-three-to-four-year check-in, and we had been told it was time to get more information on whatever was happening with our daughter.

Although the work of preparing for an overseas trip felt daunting at this particular time of life, I could not wait to fall into the arms of my mother and get some sweet relief. Share my child with her, but also take a nap. A long nap. Or maybe many long naps all in a row.

I boxed up all of our possessions, which, while relatively few in comparison to many, felt like a big job during this particular stage of life. We'd decided to let our apartment go and put our things in storage as we were busting out the seams of our tiny

Asian apartment and could not figure out how to add a new member of the family to this envelope of a space.

I was looking forward to a bigger apartment. I was excited at the prospect of choosing a home that would suit our family's needs as we now had actual children that would grow and go to school and make friends and become their own little people in this city and country that has allowed us to put down roots.

The flight back to the US went surprisingly smoothly.

What did not go smoothly was what all went down on the other end, in a place where everything was supposed to feel easier.

Within forty-eight hours, my go-getter mother had called in the troops. Her living room was crowded with therapists and teachers she had worked with in the public schools who had come to examine my daughter. They were writing many things on very oversized pieces of paper and charts. I watched as they asked her to perform various tasks.

I felt like this test was the biggest one of our lives.

They all agreed we should start working on extremely big lists of things immediately, and the trips to the doctor that followed felt much the same. We were thrown into a whirlwind that we didn't know to expect.

As much as I was relieved to be speaking English, it wasn't as much of a help as I thought it would be, as many of the words they were tossing around didn't mean anything to me. Symptoms included hypotonia, eosinophilic esophagitis, amblyopia, and more I couldn't even pronounce. We were sent to doctors with specialties I had never heard of before: gastroenterology and endocrinology. When a doctor asked us why we hadn't seen a geneticist yet, I was utterly confused. Why should we? What do they do? I would find out what a geneticist was very soon and then be in constant communication with one for the following ten years.

Learning that our baby girl had a life-long genetic syndrome that affected every cell in her body and caused ongoing medical complications and an intellectual disability rocked our world. We suddenly found ourselves with a few helpful answers for our struggles, but a million more questions and a massive pile of appointments at the hospital. The big one. The hospital reserved for kids that were in dire straits.

Our life was continuing on across the ocean, but we were not there to live it. We were straddling the two worlds, but I kept needing to put more and more weight on my American foot to make sure I didn't topple over. China continued to be what came next, but next never seemed to happen. The right now just never seemed to end.

When I boarded that plane to return to the USA from China, I had no idea that I wouldn't be back.

Slowly we discovered ourselves needing to find a place to live and a job and a church and learning how to be adults in the US for the first time after living a decade in China, all while navigating a medical system and making tough choices about our daughter's health and life.

And then, one day, we realized that we weren't going back.

It ripped the carpet out from right under my feet. I expected to spend a lifetime in Tibet. Instead, I accidentally arrived back in the US only seven years after leaving.

This was not the way it was supposed to go.

We left China and Tibet and all of the people we thought we'd know for a lifetime. But we also left dreams and hopes that we loved and cared about and had assumed were ours to keep.

I never considered, never even had a fleeting thought, that outside circumstances could be big enough and strong enough to take those dreams entirely and never give them back.

Before I pour out my heart all over these following few pages and let you in on how it all happened, I need to say something first.

I wouldn't change how things turned out.

Not even a smidge.

Even though our daughter's situation was the catalyst that brought us back to an unexpected life in the US, it's a life we are glad to call ours and wouldn't have it any other way. Our daughter is cherished, and I would sacrifice any dream if it meant I got her. She is loved and wanted, and losing China is the smallest price to pay to love her the best way I can.

Furthermore, back then, I couldn't see the new dreams waiting for me in a life I couldn't imagine. I couldn't see that sometimes the dreams most worth having are not the ones that you work for and plan for, but the ones that fall into your lap and force you to walk with them whether you want to or not.

I have a good life. A great life. I have a loving husband and a perfect daughter, and a son who has brought more joy to our lives than I could ever have imagined.

My days can be hard and complicated. A medical diagnosis hangs around our neck and follows us around day and night. But my days are also filled with joy and love. Disability has opened up to us a world we had never set foot in, and what a world worth visiting. There's a place at the table for me here, in this place, that I didn't even know existed back when I was thick in the wilds of China's Tibet.

And I'm so glad I didn't miss out.

Life didn't turn out the way I thought it would. But, whose life does?

My days are full of good things, and I know God loves me, and I am happy. The benefits I have in my life and the losses I endured cannot be pitted against each other. They are superglued together, and I have made all of the peace in my heart that I need to make over the way that works. We are content to live out this story exactly as it has been written.

But losing something that you thought was yours to have is incredibly confusing. At that time, I could not imagine a life that did not involve China and Tibetans. I had no plan B. Ever. And so when plan A was just gone, in an instant, I was so very, very lost. There were no roads to walk, no place to grab, no dreams to smile at or hold or run towards.

It felt wrong and baffling and sad. Really sad. The why questions were relentless. How could this be God's plan? I think the confusion was exaggerated because it felt like God had given me this specific dream, and I had accepted it. I took this heavy dream and placed it on my back and in my arms, tucked it deep inside my soul, and said, "Okay. Your dream is my dream."

And then to have Him take it back felt cruel and unfair and not too far from flat-out betrayal.

We took a decade of hard work and dumped it all down the drain.

At least, that's what it looked like on my worst days. It felt like a waste.

That's the painful part, right? All of this work that was all meant to compile and produce some miraculous result at the end was suddenly hit by a gust of wind and scattered everywhere and nowhere and forgotten, and then it's just gone. All gone.

One big, stinking waste.

We can't say for sure that even one person came to a saving knowledge of Jesus Christ after all of that.

After all of those years living in China, we could speak the language of the people. The Chinese people and the Tibetan people. We could talk about the Bible and the God-above-all-gods and laugh and love and hope with the people of that place. We had grown used to their food and customs and felt comfortable moving among them. We had deep friendships and opportunities, and we saw doors open and buds foreshadowing the fruit that felt just around the corner. The path before us felt solid and sure and bright and beautiful.

And then the path disappeared. It just stopped, and no matter if we looked to the left or the right or anywhere in-between, there was nowhere to put our feet. The road ended.

I want to know why I gave so many years to a people and a

place and to serve God in that way, only for Him to say, that's enough now.

There are days when I think I see it. I think I can see the beautiful significance that has emerged from all of the hard and the hurt and the loss.

On other days that moment of clarity doesn't come at all. I squint, and I scrunch up my eyes, begging for a bit or a piece or a glimmer of something or anything, but I'm just not seeing it.

I can name quite a few good things that have happened due to us leaving behind the life we had in China. Is any of them THE REASON why it was God's time for us to go? Was there one particular thing God wanted to accomplish through this whole big thing? Or is the story wide and big and full and complicated?

Maybe it's about the journey, not the destination.

Maybe it's more about what God does in me and not about what God does through me.

Or maybe it's about any other thing we throw around to help us muddle through confusing circumstances.

Maybe they are all true.

Maybe it just is what it is.

And that is the exact place where I find faith. Believing and trusting that all of it matters, but also knowing that I don't have to have *how* it all matters or fits together figured out. That the same freedom I've found in letting my insides match my outsides can also be found in accepting what I don't know just as much as accepting what I do know.

Let be what is, and let the questions, doubts, and unknowns sit there for what they are, out in the open, not explaining them away but learning to live alongside them. Stop trying to make it all fit neatly into the box with a bright shimmery bow and perfect packaging. Instead, letting the confusion seep outside the lines and letting what I understand and what I don't and what feels hard and sad blur into what is good and joyful and create the picture of what truly is. To look back on what could have been and what was and what is and know that He was there and He is here.

And I just say, "Okay."

CHAPTER 33

God gave me seven glorious years in Tibet. Hindsight has made those years look like glittering jewels, even though we all know there was much more to the story than glittering jewels. There is always more to any story than glittering jewels.

Life is a series of moments. Tiny moments all stacked on top of each other that create lives and stories and communities and whole worlds of spaces. Sometimes moments feel huge and sometimes small, but after time passes, you often can't even tell which ones really were huge and which ones were really small anyway.

In each moment, we have choices to make.

A choice to love or give or listen or sit or rest or even run the other way.

When we arrived back in the US and had given birth to our son, we stayed in someone else's picturesque American home while we tried to figure out our next steps in this life that suddenly seemed to have turned itself on its head. This beautiful home had a wrap-around porch, espresso machine, beautiful quilts, and central air.

About as far from where we had come as you could get.

I struggled in the middle of such comfort, knowing that this life in suburbia would somehow soon be mine again. Luxury that I had wished for when we were in China now left me frustrated and angry because it felt forced upon me.

I wished to hear the noise of the city's bicycle bells, the steamed buns vendor raising his voice to draw in customers, or even the Chinese pop music being blared from speakers on the street that used to drive me bananas. I never wanted any of that until I couldn't have it anymore.

I felt that all that was big and grand and vital had been lost, and I was left standing there trying to manage what was small and trivial and inconsequential.

I looked around me at the piles of laundry, the vomit I was scrubbing out of the carpet, and the vacuum cleaner I had turned on to see if it would help me lull the crying baby who was strapped to me to sleep as I swayed him back and forth and scrubbed and cried right along with him.

I stopped what I was doing and quietly screamed in a whisper, "How did a girl who used to ride horses to nomad camps in the Tibetan plateau get here?"

I held my breath, put my face in my hands, and stopped.

I stopped and sat and then let out my breath when I couldn't last any longer.

God.

The answer to my question was emblazoned upon my heart, mind, and soul, and I wept.

God. The answer was that God Himself was how I got here.

God had led me to this moment, to this place, to this circumstance.

And I had a choice. What would I do with this moment that God had given me?

Just as much as God had called me to Tibetans and to serve Him in China, He had called me to this moment, to this room, to care for a sick child and a colicky newborn. Just as much.

Could I hang up that part of me that traveled to distant shores, spoke other languages, and told the least-reached about a Savior's love for them?

Could I give it up and be content?

Here's what I decided.

Only God gets to choose what's big or small.

My task was simple and clear-cut. It was only to obey.

And obedience meant to love God and love people, the people that were right here, snuggled up next to me, needing milk and hugs and diaper changes and therapy and doctor appointments. And one last thing. Don't forget to keep my eyes on Jesus while I did it.

That, I could do.

Not perfectly, but somehow.

God has shown me that I can be content to call this story mine. All of it. Whatever it looked like before, whatever it looks like now, and whatever it will look like ten years from now and beyond. It's a story that has made me who I am and a story that has helped me grasp just a little bit more of who God is.

Back then, leaving China felt like a total break. A then-versus-now. A rift in time.

But from where I'm sitting now, the two worlds have collided. I carry with me those years and those lessons and those people. The influence those years of chasing faith among yaks and nomads still have on my life is startling. My experiences during that time are rooted and entwined so completely into my identity that they still whisper their way into my thoughts and actions daily as I go about living my suburban Minnesota life.

I know that while I'm over here helping my kids brush their teeth with their Buzz Lightyear and Cinderella toothbrushes and putting on their soft pajamas, ShiDa is rising from her bed to sweep the floor and boil potatoes harvested from her garden.

And as I say a prayer for my girl as I lay her down to sleep, I think of the painter's daughter and her mother, helping her daughter rise and get dressed and walk another day.

And as I accept the new dreams that God has given me, I trust that God will fill the hearts of others with dreams of Tibet, just as he did for me, before any single one of those Tibetans had become a real person in my life.

And I trust that all of those whose lives we knew will remember that we love them, but so much more so loved by the God-above-all-gods, who loved us so deeply that when we had lost our way to Him, He sent His only Son to rescue us.

We never thought we would one day say goodbye. We never pictured a life apart from the noise of our Chinese city apartment or the silence of the Jangka hills, or across the ocean from those that had become so near and dear to our hearts.

There are days when I'm desperate to know that my shortened years of serving God in a foreign land meant something, even after all of the sweet lessons God has worked into my heart.

I struggle to know if I made perfectly-right choices or perfectly-wrong choices or choices that landed somewhere in the middle as I stepped through villages and lives and crowded streets.

I'm sure now that I didn't get it all right. But I'm not sure I got it all wrong, either.

Maybe there's no need to figure out what went right or what went wrong, because sometimes what went wrong leads to what went right in the end, anyway.

Maybe I got in God's way. Perhaps I opened His way.

Maybe God is bigger than all that.

One thing I am certain of is that God was with me more surely than anything else I know. I felt His presence envelop me as much as I felt my own skin as I lived and moved among the Tibetan and the Chinese.

So maybe it's enough to say He was there with me.

Because if He was there with me, then He was there with them, too.

When I left those snow-covered mountain peaks and those gloriously unique people that had become so vibrantly alive before my eyes for the very last time, I left behind some of me there, for sure.

And I have to believe that means I left some of Him there, too.

ACKNOWLEDGMENTS

I'm so grateful for my husband and kids, who cheered me on and believed in both my dream and in me. If I could choose any family in the world to be mine, I'd choose you.

I am forever grateful to my parents, who gave me knowledge and love of Jesus and the ministry life from an early age. You have both been examples to me from my earliest memories until now.

To Nance, who tirelessly met with me throughout this entire project - to keep me on track, problem-solve, and coach me all the way to the finish line. Your wisdom, grace, and friendship are all things I cherish alongside my very most treasured things.

To all of those who physically walked alongside me as the moments written in this book unfolded, you will always be lodged in my heart. An extra thank you to those who took it upon themselves to read the manuscript of Chasing Faith and offer insights, suggestions, and help. I cannot thank you enough for blessing me in this way and offering the readers a clearer and more accurate picture of these years.

A very special thanks to Pastor Jim, who selflessly supported this work with his knowledge of words and the intricacies of the English language. You and Jill were there for us in so many ways as we transitioned back into America, and it was very special to share the culmination of this project with you.

To those at Central Asia Publishing, I am most grateful for the work you do to love God and love people in all of the nooks and crannies of the globe. I am so grateful for the care, help, support, and work you put in to make this dream a reality. May you be blessed in future endeavors.

To the Tibetans of Jangka, thank you for showing me how to both give and receive love. You are beautiful inside and out. I will never forget you.

And finally, to the God-above-all-gods. This one's for you.